I KILLED

Joumana Haddad

# I Killed Scheherazade

Confessions of an Angry Arab Woman

**SAQI**

ISBN: 978-0-86356-427-7

First published by Saqi Books in 2010

A full CIP record for this book is available from the British Library.
A full CIP record for this book is available from the Library of Congress.

Manufactured in Lebanon

**SAQI**

26 Westbourne Grove, London W2 5RH, UK
2398 Doswell Avenue, Saint Paul, Minnesota, 55108, USA
Verdun, Beirut, Lebanon
**www.saqibooks.com**

To my daughter,
The one I might/might never have,
Awaited, unexpected,
Wanted, feared,
Dreamed, held in arms,
Made of hope, made of flesh,
Real, unbelievable,
With a thousand names
Yet forever unnamed,
Born,
Unborn,
Loved in both her forests.

# Contents

'The Arab malaise is inextricably bound with the gaze of the Western Other – a gaze that prevents everything, even escape. Suspicious and condescending by turns, the Other's gaze constantly confronts you with your apparently insurmountable condition. You have to have been the bearer of a passport of a pariah state to know how categorical such a gaze can be. You have to have measured your anxieties against the Other's certainties about you to understand the paralysis it can inflict.'

Samir Kassir
*Being Arab*

# Note to the Reader

The idea of this book started with a foreign journalist asking me, one rainy day in December 2008, how did an 'Arab woman like you reach the point of publishing a controversial erotic magazine like *JASAD* in Arabic?' Were there any particular elements and precursors in my upbringing and background, she inquired, that paved the way for such an 'uncommon' and polemic decision?

'Most of us in the West are not familiar with the possibility of liberated Arab women like you existing,' she added.

She had meant it as a compliment, of course, but I remember being provoked by her words and rather rude in my reply: 'I don't think I am that exceptional. There are many "liberated Arab women" like me. And if you are not aware that we exist, as you claim, then it is your problem not ours.'

Later that evening, I regretted my defensive reaction. Still, the journalist's question remained stuck in my head, and I tried to understand better why she had asked it, and why it had irritated me to that extent. My attempt to understand soon became a small text; the small text developed into a long piece; the long piece then grew to become an exposé; the exposé combined with other texts I had produced around the same subject on various previous occasions; it all merged with some pertinent and revealing autobiographical notes I had written over the years; and the result was a book: this book.

Was it a good or a bad idea? Is it necessary or irrelevant? Too general? Too personal? Too scattered? Too self-absorbed? It's rather late for me to ask these, and similar, questions now. The only thing I know is that writing it felt inevitable. Inescapable, even. Much like a love story. And to me at least, that is enough of a justification.

However, having decided to publish it, I hope I'll find more justifications for it day after day, through the new life you, the readers, are going to give it.

Dear Jenny, please accept my very late apology for my needless rudeness towards you. I hope you can consider this modest testimony as a not-too-awkward attempt to say: 'I'm sorry.'

And, most importantly: 'Thank you.'

# Foreword

*Etel Adnan*

The latest news is that Scheherazade is dead, assassinated! Was it an act of passion or of reason? Probably both. Joumana Haddad has just killed the heroine from *The Arabian Nights*. And never has a crime been so joyous – and moral.

The story of this killing is a stormy wind that clears the sky. Not the sky charged with monotheisms, but the sky that is a woman's body, the personal body that belongs only to itself.

A historical myth had to be killed so the body, and therefore also the mind, could be liberated, and this experience had to be written so it could be better affirmed.

So, before listening to noise, we must listen to silence. Before sonorous words, there is the first word, the existence of the body, and Haddad proposes, not that we lose ourselves in its glorification, but that we listen to it.

I like this narrative-cum-analysis that resonates like jazz or rap music. And yet it is an indictment of impeccable logic punctuated by anger, by more than anger, by the ecstatic – mystical – search for absolute liberation, which would be possible only through the liberation of this 'object–subject' that is this body with which life begins and ends.

But from birth the body is mired in a social context, and it is thus that the constraints begin and lead us even into slavery.

Haddad rejects mild measures. Coming from a country where there has been much killing (and for nothing), she employs equally intense violence, but of a different nature. She strikes out against all taboos and her 'crime' becomes a birth, an act of life.

She speaks of the Arab woman, of what is familiar to her, but what she says concerns all women throughout history, especially those of the Mediterranean region, where they are told with sacred authority that they are a sub-product of Creation, God having created Adam whereas Eve merely emerged from his rib. But Haddad brings the good news that woman comes only from herself, and that she must make herself, must create herself – just like man. She must become the new Scheherazade, writing her tales to participate in the creation of the world through literature.

She brings the crucial questions of identity and of taking root back, not to the social me, which is more narcissistic than we think, but to the freedom she discovered as a child, and which is the shifting place of perpetual departure.

All of this is put into question with a wild joy and a surplus of intelligence that carry us along, in a text that in the end is a barbaric poem.

It takes genius to attain such radical freedom.

# To Start With ...

*On camels, belly dancing, schizophrenia
and other pseudo-disasters*

Dear Westerner,

Allow me to warn you right from the start: I am not known for making lives any easier. So if you are looking here for truths you think you already know, and for proofs you believe you already have; if you are longing to be comforted in your Orientalist views, or reassured in your anti-Arab prejudices; if you are expecting to hear the never-ending lullaby of the clash of civilisations, you'd better not go any further. For in this book, I will try to do everything that I can to 'disappoint' you. I will attempt to disillusion you, disenchant you, and deprive you of your chimeras and ready-to-wear opinions. How? Well, simply by telling you that:

Although I'm a so-called 'Arab woman', I, and many other

women like me, wear whatever we like to wear, go wherever we wish to go, and say whatever we want to say;

Although I'm a so-called 'Arab woman', I, and many other women like me, are not veiled, subdued, illiterate, oppressed, and certainly not submissive;

Although I'm a so-called 'Arab woman', no man forbids me, or many other women like me, from driving a car, a motorcycle, a six-wheeler (or a plane, for that matter!);

Although I'm a so-called 'Arab woman', I, and many other women like me, attained high levels of education, have a very active professional life, and an income higher than that of many Arab (*and Western*) men we know;

Although I'm a so-called 'Arab woman', I, and many other women like me, do not live in a tent, do not ride camels, and do not know how to belly dance (don't feel offended if you belong to the 'enlightened camp': some still have this image of us, despite the open globalised world of the twenty-first century);

And, last but not least, although I'm a so-called 'Arab woman', I, and many other women like me, look a lot like ... YOU!

Yes, we look a lot like you, and our lives are not that different from yours. Furthermore, if you stare long enough at the mirror, I'm quite certain you'll see our eyes twinkling in your face.

We look a lot like you, yet we are different. Not because
you're from the West, and we are from the East. Not because
you're an Occidental, and we are Oriental. Not because
you write from left to right, and we write from right to left.
We are different, because all human beings on the face of
this Earth are different. We are different, as much as you
are different from your next-door neighbour. And this is
what makes life interesting. Or else we would all be bored
to death.

At least I know I would be.

Accordingly, don't let yourself be intrigued by me, or by this
book, for the wrong reasons: I am not interesting because
I am an 'Arab'. I am not interesting because I am an 'Arab
woman'. And I'm certainly not interesting because I am
an 'Arab woman writer'. (*What a disastrous classification,
especially for a label-phobic like me.*) The only good reason to
read me, the only good reason I should be interesting to you,
the only good reason any human being should be interesting
at all, is because he or she are themselves, not just a flashy
intriguing tag that they are supposed to represent.

So instead of surrendering right away to the given image
that has been shaped by someone else on your behalf, try
to ask yourself: 'What is an "Arab woman", anyway?'

This book is a modest attempt to reflect upon this issue.

It does not pretend to give answers to the questions posed, nor solutions to the problems exposed, nor lessons and formulas to abide by. Its key aspiration is to offer both a testimony and a meditation on what being an Arab woman does and *could* mean today. Its second aspiration is to achieve the first, away from the dull dryness of rhetorical speech, from the narrow egocentrism of a systematic autobiography, and from the escapist allegories of a novel.

Yet, dear Westerner, don't be misled by the fact that you are the obvious addressee of this book: it is not solely addressed to you, but rather, and sometimes even primarily, to my fellow Arab citizens. Therefore it is, to a large extent, an effort of self-criticism. And while it will try to reveal the points where hope for today's Arab women lies, it will similarly expose their points of weakness, the challenges they are confronting, and the problems that they are facing/ provoking/not dealing with. Occasionally, this movement of high and low tides between depicting and condemning our harsh reality, and trying to prove there is a sure light out there, might produce an effect of self-contradiction; for how can one support a vision while denigrating its underground? But this effect is merely an illusion, and the direct result of critical integrity. No effort of self-defence deserves to be taken seriously if it is not accompanied, and sustained, by an effort of self-criticism. If I unmercifully expose our flaws, it is to better enlighten the undeniable exception that lies within them.

And vice versa.

෧෨

'Stories *only* happen to those who are able to tell them' (Paul Auster). However, in order to be able to tell some of my stories, and ponder on what being an Arab woman really means today, I'd first need to sum up some of what being an Arab signifies.

Being an Arab today implies, first and foremost – yet without generalisation – mastering the Art of 'Schizophrenia'.

Why? Because being an Arab today means you need to be a hypocrite. It means you cannot live and think what you really want to live and think honestly, spontaneously and candidly. It means you are split in two, forbidden from speaking the blunt truth (*and the truth IS blunt; such is its role, and this is its power*), because the Arab majority depends upon a web of comforting lies and illusions. It means that your life and your stories must be repressed, clamped-down and encoded; rewritten to suit the vestal guardians of Arab chastity, so the latter can rest assured that the delicate Arab 'hymen' has been protected from sin, shame, dishonour or flaw.

Obscurantists are multiplying in our Arab culture like fungi, and we come across their shadows everywhere, in every issue. Their minds are parasitic; and likewise are their hearts, souls and bodies. They can only survive as ticks. Their business is to distort and crush anything free, creative or beautiful that has escaped their hypocrisy and superficiality. Wherever freedom, creativity and beauty manage to shine forth, they release waves of hostility and resentment; they launch campaigns of distortion and untruth, in order to destroy what has broken away from their mediocrity.

I repeat, obscurantists are multiplying in our culture like fungi, and are generating mountains of menaces, aggressions, demagoguery, charlatanism and double-standards. These 'soldiers of chastity' defend ethics, although ethics cannot but wash its hands clean of them. They pretend to guard values, while real human values have nothing to do with them. They claim to protect, with their sick and twisted minds, what they dare to call honour, faith, dignity and morality, clamouring for the need to 'save our religion, customs, traditions and youth'; all while overlooking what is unfolding on television screens, through the internet, behind closed doors, and even in places of worship. They only understand the very tip of the iceberg of honour and morality, and merely grasp the superficial.

These 'thieves' have robbed us of our personal lives: they have stolen our individual freedoms and our civil liberties (*the right to live freely, the right to choose freely, the right to express freely*). They have embezzled our culture, and have desecrated and murdered it: as they have done with our future, civility, and illuminist Arab heritage. And the list of their vandalisms goes on.

These backward-looking obscurantists are thieves. They are desecrators. They are murderers. And, on top of everything, they are *stupid*. And this is perhaps the cruellest blow to our contemporary Arab identity.

Secondly, being an Arab today means being part of a herd; completely surrendering your individuality, and blindly following behind a leader, a cause or a slogan. "Nations are built by the masses," the Arab motto says. This, perhaps, is what has reinforced my scepticism towards groups, ideologies and collective struggles – even those that espouse noble causes – and my attachment to my own individuality: a 'humanitarian' individuality which respects, recognises and takes into account the other's existence and needs, but that stands firmly against any homogenising tendencies.

Surely, the herd mentality is not strictly and exclusively an Arab problem, especially not in this era of populism. We

have unfortunately witnessed so many nations, even in so-
called developed countries, fall into the same 'follow the
leader even if he's a jerk' trap: how else could we explain
America's George W. Bush, to mention but one example out
of many? Yet in the Arab world (at least the contemporary
one, to be fair to our great legacy), this disease is not just
a 'dim episode of history', but a permanent condition. For
this world is blind to the fact that all groups are the sum of
their individuals, and that if these groups are not built upon
the person as he or she is, in thought, in action, in feeling,
in body, spirit and mood, then they will self-destruct, and
become more like flocks being led by instinct and power,
unaware of their own will, with the logic of 'the group over
the individual'.

I know exactly what, in our dark Arab political, social
and cultural realities, phrases like 'groups over individuals' mean. Under such a pretext, the masses are organised
and controlled, herded into different crowds that eradi-
cate any personal aspect: whether it is opinion, choice,
feeling, temper, understanding, expression, ambition or
life altogether. The individual is subsumed into factions
based on the general social, religious and political trends,
tamed and de-clawed of his/her uniqueness by the authorities. Practically and objectively, this leads to the dissolving
of all individual talent under the wave of the crushing,

homogenising collective entity. Individuals melt in the furnace, see their egos obliterated, forbidden from playing any creative role; which contributes to promoting the reigning clichés about Arabs, and the stereotyped image of them. The more we assemble to make our voices heard, the more our discourse is misunderstood. Can you top the viciousness of this vicious circle?

But what purpose is there to life, and what dignity to any group, to any collective strife, if the 'I' is crushed under the hooves of the herd? Don't get me wrong: I am not defending good old-style individualism here. I do not mean the 'Darwinist' approach, based on the 'homo homini lupus' ideology, which has primarily produced a selfish, unfair and destructive society, where there is no place for the weak and the poor, and no communal and environmental awareness. This model is as inept and damaging as the failed socialist model which, in the name of beautiful egalitarian ideas, has crushed individuals, their freedoms, their dreams and their lives.

What I am talking about is finding a balance in the middle: a balance that so many people are striving and fighting for, and that would be the efficient and noble product of an efficient and noble competition between Capitalism and Communism. Much like the balance that some Northern European countries have succeeded in finding, to a large extent at least.

*"Liberté, Égalité, Fraternité"*: more than 220 years later, and we're not there yet ...

But it still sounds like the best option, wouldn't you agree?

Being an Arab today means thirdly, and this is my last point, facing an endless series of impasses: the impasse of totalitarianism; the impasse of political corruption; the impasse of favouritism; the impasse of unemployment; the impasse of poverty; the impasse of class discrimination; the impasse of sexism; the impasse of illiteracy; the impasse of dictatorial regimes; the impasse of religious extremism; the impasse of misogyny, polygamy and homophobia; the impasse of financial fraud; the impasse of hopelessness, emptiness and lack of purpose; the impasse of the Middle East conflict; the impasse of the Palestinian tragedy; the impasse of the West's partiality; the impasse of the West's hostility, fear, arrogance, suspicion, condescension ... etc.

You see, being an Arab and living in the Arab world today is like banging your head on a thick wall made of steely political, social and existential predicaments. You hammer and hammer, yet nothing changes. Except the number of bruises on your skin. But you have to keep on banging that wall from the inside. That is your only hope. For it cannot be wrecked, penetrated or torn down from the outside.

And especially not by 'outsiders'. Change is not 'importable' material.

ﻋﻭ

"The Arab human being suffers from the schizophrenia disease: a collective schizophrenia which we all live, divided between what we are told to believe and what we do believe, between what we say and what we do. But the time has come to start naming things by their real names and assuming their responsibility," writes Tunisian theatre actress and writer Jalila Bakkar. Having tried to summarise some of what being an Arab means at the present time (the schizophrenia, the herd syndrome, the stalemate: three gloomy facts shared by men and women alike), I will attempt subsequently, and throughout this hybrid book, to explain what being an Arab woman suggests on the one hand (i.e. all the narrow, wrong prejudices linked to that connotation, as well as the truths shared by the bearers of this problematic identity), and on the other, what kind of responsibility it entails, and what it could truly mean (i.e. the potential positive reality, or realities, achievable despite the existing troubles and challenges).

Yet before asking: 'what is an Arab woman?' we need to

ask another question first: how is a typical Arab woman perceived in the eyes of the non-Arab? Isn't it a perception mainly formed in the Western collective consciousness by a multitude of formulas and generalisations, generated either by a still-persisting Orientalist perspective, or by a post-9/11 hostile view shaped by resentment, fear and condescension?

Isn't this woman often seen as a poor helpless female, who is condemned from birth to grave unconditionally to obey the men of the family: father, brother, husband, son, etc? As a powerless soul who doesn't have any control over her destiny? As a defenceless body told when to live, when to die, when to breed, when to hide, when to fade away? As an invisible face masked by layers of fear, vulnerability and ignorance, and utterly cancelled by the Islamic hijab? Or worse: by the Sunni burqa and the Shiite chador? A woman who is not allowed to think, speak or work for herself; who is only able to talk when she is told to, and is largely humiliated and ignored when she does speak; a woman, in short, who has no place and no dignity in humanity.

Of course, not all clichés are completely erroneous. Not all truisms are totally untrue. The Arab woman above does exist. Not only does she exist, but in order to be sincere, and scientifically precise, I have regretfully to admit that she is increasingly the ruling model of Arab women nowadays.

Wherever you go, from Yemen to Egypt, from Saudi Arabia to Bahrain, you'll find that the religious powers; the indifferent, corrupt and/or complicit political systems; the patriarchal societies; and even the Arab woman herself (for she is her own best adversary, often a co-conspirator against her sex), are excellent at innovating ways to humiliate the woman, to frustrate her and annul her own identity and role.

Yet, while admitting this fact, it does not make it less scandalous, and sad, and unfair, that almost no other image of the Arab woman is present in the West's common gaze and perception.

Again, I am not hereby generalising. Quite the contrary: I know perfectly well that the Occidental, who is aware of the mosaic, complex and heterogeneous nature of our Arab societies and cultures, does exist. The problem is that he, or she, is literally the exception that confirms the rule.

How many times, for example, have I had to explain to a surprised Western audience, in this third millennium, that yes, many Arab women do wear sleeveless tops and even miniskirts instead of head scarves, abayas (cloaks) and niqabs; and that no, the desert has had absolutely no influence on my poetic expression, simply because there is no desert in Lebanon.

An endless series of misunderstandings and oversimplifica-tions, reinforced either by widespread fear of the famous 'Arab terrorist'; or by sheer ignorance and lack of curiosity towards us; or by the mass media's fascination with the superficial/sensational side of any news (like the story of Noujoud, the 10-year-old Yemeni girl married by force by her parents; or the story of Lubna, the Sudanese journalist arrested and whipped for wearing trousers).

As the famous saying goes: 'one falling tree makes more noise than a whole forest growing.' When will we start paying attention to the whispering of a growing tree?

Undoubtedly, migration from Third-World Arab countries to Europe has also played an important role in spreading the above-cited misinterpretations, because of the 'veil reaction': i.e. the increasing number of Arab female émigrés, and Euro-pean women of Arab/Muslim origin, who are now adopting the veil as a defensive/offensive reaction to the West's – at least apparent – hostility towards Islam in the post-9/11 era. Such a visible reaction is bound to overshadow, if not totally eclipse, the 'other' Arab woman living in the West: i.e. the unveiled one, who is visually indistinguishable from Western women. As a result, the only remaining notice-able model, the only 'evident' model of the Arab woman, becomes the veiled one, with all the negative connotations that this model (justly or unjustly) carries.

Let's be fair though: the West is not the only party responsible for these misperceptions. We Arabs are guilty of distorting our image as well. Trapped in a vicious circle of defence/offence, we have done, and keep on doing, almost everything we can to encourage intolerance towards us, and promote the false images and clichés that are spread about our societies and cultures.

In short: we are talented at being our own worst enemy.

ॐ

'For most of history, Anonymous was a woman' (Virginia Woolf), and this is certainly true of Arab women. Nevertheless, the 'non-anonymous' Arab woman is no myth; the 'other', atypical, rebellious, independent, modern, freethinking, unconventional, highly educated, self-sufficient Arab woman exists as well. Moreover, she is not as uncommon as you might suppose.

And there lies the key to this testimony, which is nothing but a small link in a long chain of works and essays already written about this topic. Its aim lies not in proving that the prevalent image of the typical Arab woman is all wrong. But in showing that it is *incomplete*. And in placing next to it the 'other' image, so that the latter becomes an intrinsic part of the West's (and of the Arab world's) common perception of Arab women in general.

Yes, the 'other' Arab woman most certainly exists. She needs to be noticed. She deserves to be acknowledged. And I am here to tell her story, or at least one of her many stories: mine.

# I

# An Arab Woman
# Reading the Marquis de Sade

> Books are the only place in the world where two strangers
> can meet on very intimate terms.
>
> *May Ziade*
> Lebanese poet and essayist (1886–1941)

I have always been what you would call, whether sympathet-
ically or disapprovingly, a 'bad girl'. In fact, my most vivid
memory of myself growing up is of an unstoppably curious
child waiting impatiently for her parents to get out of the
house, so that she could place a chair in her father's immense
library, climb it, and reach for whatever was hidden on the
top shelves. In the earlier stages of my life, I used to think
that only two things were worth doing whenever I had the

chance of being alone: reading and masturbating. Both needed solitude in order to be fully enjoyed.

My mother likes to recall three things from my childhood that she believes to be of great significance as far as my character is concerned: a few hours after I was born, I already had my eyes wide open, she claims, greedily watching the world around me. The nurses assured her that they had rarely seen a newborn so alert to the outside world, and so famished for it.

Secondly, ever since I was nine months old, I fiercely resisted doing anything against my will: whether it was wearing the tight red coat that deprived me of free movement, or drinking milk when I wasn't really hungry. It is alleged that I scratched, bit and even spat when I had to, in order to fight back.[1]

And thirdly my mother tells the strange story that, before I could even walk, and every time she needed to get out of the house to do some errands, but had nobody to watch over me, she used to place me in a tiny chair, then put the chair on top of a high table, and leave me there, alone in the house, being certain that I would not move, because she knew, that I knew, that if I did move, I would hurt myself badly. She'd come back and find me exactly as she had left

---

1. The scratching and biting techniques, I kept. But I have since given up spitting.

me, sitting carefully on that small wooden chair, safe and sound, most probably dreaming my way to the world.

Insatiability, insubordination and awareness: three main features of my early personality which have stuck with me along the road of life – and I hope that I can assert this without sounding over-confident or self-indulgent. I do not know if these three reminiscences should be put down to the tendency of mothers to mystify their children, or to the actual truth, but what I do know is that the same greedy newborn with her green wide-open eyes; the same rebellious infant who fought back with her teeth and nails; the same perspicacious one-year-old who knew she'd better stay put if she wanted to avoid bruises and harm, is now the woman who has consistently opted, against the logic of time and place, to live an atypical life.

Yet even the most fertile of soils wouldn't grow a tree if a seed was not planted in it. What was my 'seed'? Who was, and still is, my major mentor throughout this ongoing journey?

An omnipotent accomplice called: Literature.

'It is what you read when you don't have to that determines what you will be when you can't help it' (Oscar Wilde). Since my early adolescence, I've never dreamed, like most of my girlfriends, of Tom Cruise or Bruce Springsteen or Al Pacino or Johnny Hallyday, or even, believe it or not, of Robert De Niro. Rather, I dreamed passionately of Mayakovsky, Pavese and Gibran. I dreamed of Dostoyevsky, Salinger and Éluard. Those were the strangers that I desired and fantasised about, not the movie stars and famous pop singers. My classmates were hungry for illusions; I was hungry for dreams.

Here I need to point out that – contrary to what my life, ideas and choices might suggest – I was raised by very traditional parents (despite the intellectual father and the rather modern mother); parents who didn't even allow me, among many other embargoes, to go to the movies with my friends as a teenager. On top of that, I went to an all-girls religious school for fourteen consecutive years. This traditional upbringing was not the result of religious fanaticism, nor an underestimation of me being a girl. It was rather the consequence of fear for me 'because' I was a girl. I used to object fiercely to that fear, as in my standards, it was equal to underestimation. 'I am a female thus I am vulnerable, weak, prone to danger ... etc.'

But neither my parents' conservatism nor my school environment – both of which I denounced and struggled against merely on principle – really annoyed me, because throughout my growing-up years, I was completely and utterly enraptured by the world of books and writing. So despite this traditional upbringing and the weight of fear, I grew up free on the inside, since my readings emancipated me – and freedom, as I learned later, begins in the mind, before moving on to one's expression and behaviour.

I was a bundle of contradictions: a calm and easygoing child on the outside, and a whirlwind of mental activity on the inside; sweet, gentle and caring, but turning into a snarling lioness if anyone hurt me or took what was mine; extremely sensitive, but simultaneously extremely strong. I cheated at Scrabble with my brother, because I could not take losing (I learned to deal with that later). I was fiery, passionate, stubborn, competitive, chafed against taboos and absolutely impatient (still am!). Precocious, I didn't play with toys (I mainly despised girls' games, especially the Barbie doll and its accessories), preferring to steal thick books that were inappropriate for my age, and devour them in secret.

I loved reading for many reasons: I read to breathe; I read to live (my life as much as that of others); I read to travel away; I read to escape a brutal reality; I read to smother the explosions of the Lebanese war; I read to ignore my parents' screams and their daily arguments and sufferings; I read to feed my greed; I read to accumulate strength; I read to caress my soul; I read to slap my soul; I read to learn; I read to forget; I read to remember; I read to understand; I read to hope; I read to plan; I read to believe; I read to love; I read to desire and yearn and lust ...

And I read, especially, to be able to honour the promise that I had made myself that one day my life would be different. A promise that I did, and still do, my best to keep, for the sake of that helpless, trapped little Joumana who, between the blasts of the militias' fights outside, and the shouts of her parents' fights inside, used to fly away in her dreams, from one of Beirut's filthy shelters ...

I don't remember the first book I read. I frequently ask my dad this question, since I inherited my passion for reading from him, and he was my main 'supplier', but he doesn't remember either. I do, however, vividly remember myself as a girl, maybe nine or ten years old, sitting at the kitchen table in our little house, reading and reading and then tirelessly writing out stories like the ones I had just read (often by candlelight, because of the frequent electricity cuts during wartime). My nickname at home was 'writer *pasha*', because I wrote until my middle finger swelled (this was before the computer age).

When I discovered (or should I rather say: when I was

discovered by?) the Marquis de Sade, I was a mere twelve years old. My father's bookshelves, with all their delicious pleasures, were open to me throughout the summer holidays. I could take down whatever I pleased, in absolute freedom and without any consequences, mainly due to his absence from the house all day long, and his – misplaced – trust in me. My innocent features, which contrasted sharply with the imps in my head, were the best cover for the madness, hunger and delirium going on inside that little mind. Was he really duped, my penetratingly smart father, or did he need the illusion of that sham, like any traditional parent? I honestly don't know. But in truth my 'peaceful' features still trick many people, to this day, as to my real nature and thoughts, allowing them to build judgments based on appearances ('Oh she's such a sweet girl'), thus falling into the 'trap': *my* trap ('God help us, she's the devil!').

And I do not mind that involuntary scam. Not in the least.

ﻋﻮ

That glorious Marquis de Sade day changed me irrevocably. Consider it a simple maths problem: two trains, A and B, continents and centuries apart, but which are travelling towards each other along the same track, are bound to meet at some point of time and space. The Marquis de Sade was train A, and boy, was I train B!

That hot morning, I had just finished Balzac's *Lost Illusions* and was searching for new prey. I stood in front of the high bookshelf and began skimming the titles. Then I heard a small, yellowed book on the sixth shelf call out to me. It was titled, *Justine, or the Misfortunes of Virtue*. I was intrigued. I took it down, and opened the first pages. It was a really old book, printed in 1955, published by Jean-Jacques Pauvert (of course: who else was perversely bold enough to publish such a book in France those days?!).

I skipped over Georges Bataille's great foreword, which I returned to many years later, moving straight onto the novel. I read that fantastic and awesome story in one go, in a mixture of panic and disbelief, both hypnotised and in a numb fright, like someone who is afraid, yet fatally attracted to the object of her fear. Like someone who can't stop watching a horror movie, or riding on a rollercoaster, despite the terror it causes. *Adrenaline*. That book pumped adrenaline through my nervous system. And I kept trying to relive this sensation with every volume I read after that, so that it became one of the literary standards by which I measured a book's success or failure. In fact, the search for adrenaline, and my addiction to it, also became one of the standards of my own personal life, and of my relations with the opposite sex.

'Books can be very dangerous. The best ones should be labelled: This could change your life' (Helen Exley). I don't know how a twelve-year-old girl can read a 'dangerous' book like *Justine* and come out of it 'safe'. I don't know how that girl can go straight from Balzac to de Sade without falling into the vast abyss in between them. I don't know, in simpler terms, how I emerged unscathed from that brutal encounter (have I?), but I know that it did indeed change my life. I like to refer to it as my 'baptism by subversion'.

One book at a time, one reading at a time, and one confrontation at a time, the Marquis de Sade took over my mind. He grabbed my shoulders, looked me straight in the eyes, and said, 'Your imagination is your kingdom. Everything is allowed in your mind. EVERYTHING is possible. Throw the windows open, and don't be afraid to infringe and hallucinate.'

Indeed, the Marquis released me on that day from some of my mental shackles. And after him so did other writers who wrote as beautifully, as defiantly and as insolently as he did. To cut a long story short: I became corrupt.

And there was no going back.

ॐ

Reading 'adult' material like *Justine*, *Lolita* and *Sexus* when I was twelve, thirteen and fourteen years old did me a lot of good. I should note here that I read all of these books in

French, and not in Arabic. In fact, even though I loved the Arabic language and many of its writers (especially Gibran Khalil Gibran and the modern novelists and poets), most of my reading while growing up was in French: either of French writers, or of international authors translated into French. And anyway, it's worth pointing out here the sheer impossibility of a work like *Justine* being widely available in Arabic, or taken seriously by many Arab intellectuals, either when I was growing up or today. This in spite of an Arab culture that, a thousand years ago, produced works that were far more erotic and subversive than anything being written in the West then (or even perhaps now). I will quote from the fifteenth-century work *The Perfumed Garden* by Sheikh Nefzawi to prove my argument:

> If you desire coition, place the woman on the ground, cling closely to her bosom, with her lips close to yours; then clasp her to you, suck her breath, bite her; kiss her breasts, her stomach, her flanks, press her close in your arms, so as to make her faint with pleasure; when you see her so far gone, then push your member into her. If you have done as I said, the enjoyment will come to both of you simultaneously.
>
> Not all women have the same conformation of vulva, and they also differ in their manner of making love, and in their love for and their aversion to things. A woman of plump form and with a shallow uterus will look out for a member which is both short and thick, which will

completely fill her vagina, without touching the bottom of it; a long and large member would not suit her. A woman with a deep-lying uterus, and consequently a long vagina, only yearns for a member which is long and thick and of ample proportions, and thus fills her vagina in its whole extension; she will despise the man with a small and slender member for he could not satisfy her in coition.

It has been observed that under all circumstances small women love coitus more and evince a stronger affection for the virile member than women of a large size. Only long and vigorous members suit them; in them they find the delight of their existence and of their couch. There are also women who love the coitus only on their clitoris, and when a man lying upon them wants to get his member into the vagina, they take it out with the hand and place its gland between the lips of the vulva. I pray God to preserve us from such women!

How did we get from that early high point of liberty, of talking about sex so naturally, to our constipated present-day reality, I wonder? When did we start sliding down the hill of taboos? It is one of the questions that constantly haunts me.

So much for *Justine*. What about a book like *Lolita*, then? In an Arab world where there is an overwhelming focus on female chastity, and on girls' morally uncompromised manners and behaviour, such a book is considered, of course, outrageous. On the other hand, the Islamic practice of 'institutionalised' paedophilia is not seen as outrageous, and it is quite normal for men to marry fourteen-year-old girls. The International Centre for Research on Women now estimates that there are fifty-one million child brides in the world, and almost all of them are in Muslim countries. Consider the horrifying words of Ayatollah Khomeini, one of the most famous Islamic clerics of the twentieth century, taken from his book *Tahrir al-Wasila*:

> A man is not to have sexual intercourse with his wife before she is nine years old, whether regularly or occasionally, but he can have sexual pleasure from her, whether by touching or holding her, or rubbing against her, even if she is as young as an infant. However, had he penetrated her without deflowering her, then he holds no responsibility towards her. But if a man penetrates and deflowers the infant [...], then he should be responsible for her subsistence all her life.

Talk about depravity!

Because of all these absurd double standards, I felt fortunate to have the French language as a window to the 'forbidden'. I honestly can't imagine how poor and deprived I would have been today without the cultural gifts and privileges that French has given me (and at this level and this level alone, I dare to speak about the 'luck' of being Lebanese, Lebanon being an Arab francophone country). Aragon, Stendhal, Flaubert, Hugo, Sartre, Camus, de Beauvoir, Céline, de Musset, Sand, Colette, Genet ... And let's not forget Dostoyevsky, Gogol, Miller, Nabokov, Kafka, Yeats, Marquez, Pirandello, Poe, Rilke, Pessoa and Pavese ... I have devoured many works of these great writers in French.

᪾

The second positive effect of all this reading, after the liberation of my mind, was how it saved me from the mediocre romanticism of banal, sugary and inoffensive books, such as those that my classmates used to exchange in secret, blushing at the thought of committing the 'unspeakable'. While they got excited reading Barbara Cartland's ardent love stories that culminated, in the best-case scenario, with a 'passionate kiss' or a 'wild embrace', there I was, immersed in the impossible world of tireless orgies, priests sodomising virgins, young girls seducing fifty-year-old men, and so on and so forth. My childhood ended quite early, I suppose, if by childhood we mean an age sexually innocent and 'uncorrupted'.

It wasn't that odd, consequently, that I looked at my girl-friends in a rather condescending way. In return, they used to call me the 'shy one'. For there they were, talking about a man who smiled at them on their way to school, or describing how their acne-struck cousin held their hand under the table at the Easter family lunch, while I simply had nothing to say. I wasn't interested in 'real' boys. (I made up fervently for that initial apathy at a later stage of my life.)

Reality was so much less than what I absorbed from my beloved books: it seemed so silly, childish and, frankly, not worth my time. Plus, I was a loner. I didn't mind solitude. Amidst all those wonderful things to read, dream and write about, I profoundly enjoyed my own company, deeply convinced that each person is a crowd by him/herself. My adolescent friends took my snobbish maturity for shyness. And so I gained my reputation for being timid and innocent; a reputation which served me well at school, to be honest.

The third constructive – at least in my opinion – influence from reading such subversive books at an early age is that they nourished my erotic curiosity and fantasies, and shaped in me a non-conforming sexual imagination and libido. Exploration is an art, possibilities are endless, and taboos are made to be broken.

And that, too, has served me well in life.

ৰ৶

'The exception is always described as "anomalous". We do not want to believe it, because it is threatening' (Yusra Mukaddem). 'Anomalous' books like *Justine* unquestionably changed me, and unquestionably for the better. Had I had (I may still have) a daughter (my two wonderful sons run away from books as if they were a plague), I would most certainly have offered her all these eye-opening, mind-shaking volumes as a present on her twelfth birthday. It is in fact a piece of advice I give to women who ask me for guidance, mistakenly taking my fiery enthusiasm for a guru's kind of wisdom: books, I answer them. Don't be afraid of books, even the most dissident, seemingly 'immoral' ones. Culture is a sure bet in life, whether high, low, eclectic, pop, ancient or modern. And I am convinced that reading is one of the most important tools of liberation that any human being, and a contemporary Arab woman in particular, can exploit. I am not saying it is the ONLY tool, especially with all the new alternative – more visual, interactive and hasty – ways to knowledge, learning and growth. But how could I not be convinced of literature's power, when it has been my original emancipator? And I know that I am no exception, for many other Arab women like me owe to literature the first beginnings of the atypical females that they later became.

But then there was a war on. And that's another story.

II

# An Arab Woman
# Not Belonging Anywhere

The absence of a clear vision of the future is one of the most
tragic issues that Arabs have to deal with today.

*Fatima Mernissi*

Moroccan sociologist and writer (1941–)

All human beings have phobias. Mine is rather special. It's
not an animal or a place. It's not an activity or a situation.
It's a sound.

My phobia, believe it or not, is a sound: the horrific
sound of a whistle. Whenever I hear it, it gives me goose
bumps and makes my heart beat faster. Whenever I hear
it, even now, I look towards the horizon in a panic, to see
where the shell is coming from. To see, mostly, whether
it is going to fall on my head and the heads of my loved

ones, or not. It symbolises to me the wait for death. The annihilation of the future.

And that dreadful sound – however unfair this statement might seem – summarises Beirut for me.

I can't recall how many times, while growing up in Lebanon, I thought: 'I despise this land'; how many times I've said: 'Damn this country. Damn this homicidal identity, damn this cruel geography, damn these nasty religions that turn man against man because of a God who is uncertain of his own existence.'

I can't recall how many times I have wished, in those frequent moments of despair and misery, to have a weightless *empty* heart, without the extra load of fear, pain, sorrow, disappointment, grief, regret, frustration, doubt, resentment, mourning, suspicion ...

Many people love their childhood and cherish it. I simply loathe it, and, except for the inspiring books that enriched it and made it bearable, I'd pretty much like to forget all about it. I would not save a single detail. I cannot blame everything on the war of course: it was merely one of many destructive and aggressive elements surrounding me. But let's not fall into the easy trap of self-commiseration. It is not my style. Plus, none of the conflicts I have witnessed and experienced

succeeded in destroying me. Quite the contrary: we owe it
to wars that they turn many of us, their survivors, into fierce
fighters, with an endless appetite for life, accomplishment,
joy, knowledge and progress. Yet sometimes I cannot help
thinking: how different would we Arabs be now (whether
Lebanese, Palestinians, Iraqis, etc: take your pick) if we had
not witnessed all these dreadful wars.

War is men's business, they say. So losing loved ones
must be women's, I assume. How much more serene, more
concentrated on her own personal fights, would the Arab
woman be today if she had not been forced, in so many
countries, to occupy the position of the widowed wife or the
orphaned daughter or the distressed mother and sister?

And what about me? How much less addicted to risk
would I be today, I wonder, had I not lived what I lived
during my early years? Had I not seen, for example, the leg
of our neighbour Malcon being torn apart from his body?
Or militiamen tying adversaries to their cars, and dragging
them like dead dogs through the streets of Beirut?

'Conflict is my destiny, I need to accept it,' I used to say out
loud in front of the mirror, repeating it like a mantra just
to calm down after such a spectacle, or a nasty explosion,
or the news of a horrific assassination. I even ended up
masochistically enjoying the hideous impact of this statement on my ears, skin, lungs, stomach, pelvis, etc. I ended

up becoming used to the symphony of combat ... What a dreadful thing to say, feel and think. But it is true nevertheless. 'I'm war-broken,' I tell my foreign friends now, in an attempt to make fun of what is most hurting inside me. After so many years of training and alienation, I've become used to the symphony of combat, and used to the fear and death that come with it.

I became used to it all, that is, except the whistling.

You see, I was struck by the fatal lightning of the famous Lebanese civil war when I was only four and a half years old. It broke out in 1975. On the thirteenth of April 1975. 'Black Sunday' as it is called. When they first heard the gun blasts and explosions that day, my parents thought they were fireworks. 'Maybe it is some fancy wedding,' my mother said, and kept on cooking the Sunday meal. But it was not a fancy wedding. It was a war that consumed the best years of my childhood and adolescence. A war that killed people, destroyed homes and families, and became a factory of widows and orphans. A war that made time feel heavy and thick, almost like mud. A war that turned me all rotten inside, full of insecurities and putrid wounds that I did, and still do, my best to hide (or deal with).

And those wounds are the price of being born, like me, in Beirut.

ॐ

'Belonging has to be chosen, received and renewed. It is a lifetime's work' (John O'Donohue). At this point, I feel I need to clarify that, even though I was raised in Beirut, and even though I've never left it to live abroad, I have in no way ever felt that I belonged to it as a city and a place. Perhaps this is because I have seen its ugly, cruel, harsh face: the face of war, and destruction, and worry, and killing, and running to shelters. I did not play in its streets; I did not walk on its Corniche; and I did not live its heydays.

It wasn't until I was seventeen, for example, that I first went to West Beirut. Before that, it was just a picture on a postcard, or a vague place that my parents would talk about occasionally, when hit by nostalgia. They would also talk about Cinema Capitol, Souk El Tawileh, and other mysterious places with names that I could not relate to. My Beirut is not theirs. There was a gap, a clean cut. No connection, no build-up. I might as well be from another country, with a totally different capital ...

So Beirut is not my mother, not my friend, and not my partner. There is no love lost between us, or even complicity. She did not give birth to me, and neither of us has adopted the other. In truth, this separation, or lukewarm relationship, does not bother me at all, and I don't feel a lack in my life because of it, since I am rootless in any case, and like to think of my feet as being stuck in the clouds. My true nation is a few places that I love and find myself in, scattered all over the world. I visit them, but do not live in them; that is why they continue to surprise me and I don't stake any claim over them. This is my personal take on attachment.

When I look at Beirut today, I see a woman who has lost her identity, trapped in an endless cycle of plastic surgeries, continually staring at the mirror instead of looking into her own soul, trying to regain some of her magic, grace and past glories. Where is her heart located? I don't know. What is the rhythm of its beat? I don't know either. I am much more familiar with the city now than before, but to be honest, there are still some neighbourhoods I haven't visited, and other neighbourhoods that fluster me when I enter them. Many of my friends who lived in it before the war say that it is now artificial and false, for the most part. I cannot make this comparison, because I am not acquainted with Beirut's true self. I even wonder: does Beirut have a true self? Isn't it, as all places we live in, what we dream it to be, an amalgam of our fantasies and projected desires?

I have no fervour for Beirut, but I do have some empathy. I don't feel tenderness, or longing, or nostalgia, but maybe some kindness. It does not attract me, will not win me over, and I sense that it doesn't really like me either. But if I had to pick one side of it that I like, or to be more accurate, one that I can stand better than the others, it would be its night face. I like her darkness, her noise and her surrender to her freedom, her desires and her whims. Beirut during the daytime is overdone, but at night, she just washes her face with water and soap, and goes out without make-up or wigs. Beirut during the daytime is first and foremost a trader, but at night she turns into a vulnerable woman, and becomes more honest and transparent, thus maybe closer to her essence and meaning.

'The shock produced by the war pushed me to understand, explore and write about Beirut. Yet I believe that the most that worried me before I started writing was the question: how can I write about a city that does not resemble the one described to us in our parents' and grandparents' stories? What kind of city can I portray, while I was witnessing with my own eyes the shattering of its dream of modernity on various levels?' (Alawiya Sobh). Unlike many Lebanese writers, I've never personally felt the pull to write a book about Beirut, or inspired by her. At times my readers ask me: 'Why don't you write about the war in your poetry?'

My first answer is: 'I am not ready yet.'

My second answer is: 'I'd be ashamed to take advantage of the war in order to raise interest in my writing.'

And my third (and best) answer is: 'Don't look for the blade. It's all in the scars.'

In fact, since my early days with writing, I have always felt that my city is an anti-inspiration. And I still feel that everything I do, everything I say, everything I write, I am doing and saying and writing 'against' her will. Our relationship is polite, appropriate and cordial at most, but there is a vast degree of alienation between us. Beirut the queen of contradictions. Beirut the martyr and the whore. The veiled and the emancipated. The ambiguous and the obvious. The treacherous and the loyal. The money lover and the artist. The Oriental and the Occidental. The seductress and the pilgrim ...

The city where living is similar to acting in a TV soap opera;

Where you can't help but feel you are 'sleeping with the enemy' every time you go to bed. And that this enemy is you;

Where you have more chance of earning your living as a bartender than as a writer;

Where the only readership that you can dream of as a writer *(but not count on)* is the one constituted by your fellow authors – who obviously expect you to return the favour when their turn comes to publish a new book;

Where anarchy is considered order, and the notion of honour is strictly linked to what's between a girl's thighs;

Where all politicians are continuously quarrelling over power as chickens quarrel over a few crumbs of bread, but almost none of whom is paying attention to our need for a civil, cultured and aware society;

Where religious authorities are still the ultimate decision makers on people's private and public concerns;

Where women don't even enjoy the right to pass their nationality on to their children, if they are married to a foreigner, among many other discriminative regulations, but do benefit from a special bank loan to get their boobs blown up and their noses sized down;

Where homosexuals have to hide as if they represent a deadly plague;

Where movies can be censored in the blink of an eye if they tackle 'delicate' issues (like sex and religion);

Where we still don't have a proper museum of contemporary art;

Where it makes much more sense, for most young women, to shop or to waste a whole day tanning in the sun than to devote one hour to reading a few pages of a good book (while they could do both perfectly easily);

Where girls from 'good families' are still expected to be virgins on their wedding night;

Where guys are still looking for virgin girls from 'good families' to marry;

Where many bookshops are dying away, and several publishers are struggling to stay alive;

Where my seventeen-year-old son is still taught at school that poetry means a set of romantic phrases which rhyme at the end;

Where my ten-year-old son is more curious about Akon, 50 Cent and Tectonic dancing than about Chopin, Picasso and Victor Hugo, because the latter are unfairly introduced to him in the dullest possible way ...

I could go on forever about our faults, deficiencies and mishaps. I know that this might come as a surprise to many, since the reputation of Beirut is that of a 'different' Arab city. More open, more cosmopolitan, more egalitarian. And Beirut is indeed different. But exaggerating its particularities in the region would make us fall into the anti-cliché trap: the one that indulges itself by pretending that everything is going perfectly well in the best of all possible worlds. Well, it is not. Quite the contrary: many things are going dangerously wrong in our 'brave old world'.

I realise that this must seem rather harsh and ruthless, but I can't allow myself to criticise the Arab world without criticising, even more harshly, my own country, which is a part of it. Plus, I am convinced that patriotism is an expression of candid romanticism. And therefore it is unacceptable to me. Patriotism makes you blind. Patriotism makes you self-deceiving. Patriotism puts you in a constant state of denial. If we are not harsh in criticising ourselves, and in trying to improve, then we are allowed no expectations. I believe that most Lebanese unfortunately have a certain talent for self-indulgence. If we can't blame the war, we blame the political situation. If we can't blame the political situation, we blame the debts. If we can't blame the debts, we blame the foreign powers. If we can't blame the foreign powers, we blame the neighbouring ones. And so on and so forth. The only thing that we haven't blamed yet for our misfortunes is the weather, and we might get to that very soon, because we are running out of arguments, and global warming seems like a very good and serious one.

That is why I feel that everything I do, everything I say, everything I write, I am doing and saying and writing to defeat this perfidious mother, to crush her crushing influence over me. Like a monster that needs to be stabbed in the heart, or else it will keep on devouring a new piece of me every day until there is nothing left.

I would certainly not want to belong to such a place. Would you?

৵

At times I am asked about issues of Identity and Belonging, and what they mean to me. Well, in addition to my scepticism towards all absolute concepts, towards words that seem to be invented to be written in capital letters, I also believe that in this life there is the 'us', and then there is the vision we have of us. My vision of me – the one I like at least, since I have numerous visions, some of which are completely hideous – is of someone without an anchor. That is probably why I have a stronger sensation of belonging in faraway places than I have ever felt towards my own city. Like when I stroll the streets of Saint-Germain in Paris. Or when I contemplate the changing skies over any Italian city. Or when I walk by the seaside in Cartagena, Colombia. The sum of all these places is my true motherland. And it will always be an incomplete motherland, with new cities and places added to it each time I discover a new me in a different spot. A friend once asked me: 'What is your favourite place in the whole world?' And I immediately answered: 'My head.' So maybe my true city is just ... me!

(And the arms of the man I love, when I am in love.)

Belonging? Thanks but no thanks. I grew up in a country that hates me, and that expressed this hatred in so many ugly ways. I do not want to belong to a place like that. No, I definitely do not belong to Beirut: I just live in it. The thought of belonging to such a monstrous, murderous womb terrifies me. A womb that gives you life only to steal it away from you in different sadistic manners and techniques. I know that, as a Lebanese, and as an Arab, I am the product of that womb, but I do not fit in. It sort of spat me out and left me all alone in a jungle. So it is only natural for me to reject it, to try to hurt it by scratching it ferociously with my nails or kicking it hard with my feet.

'I must be cruel only to be kind. This bad begins, and worse remains behind' (Shakespeare, *Hamlet*). I am not cruel to Beirut. It is just that my progress through the city has been, so far, a dizzying series of bumps and clashes. However, I have to say that surviving it (because you do not live in Beirut: you survive it), and being inflexible about doing and saying things my way, have also shaped the woman that I am, and brought me a great deal of satisfaction, and a wonderful feeling of fulfilment. One happy side effect of this stubbornness is how my father, for example – that same father who did not let me out of the house on my own; who insisted on seeing nothing but a pure angel in me; who, in vain, hid all the books that he considered dangerous and corrupting on the highest shelves of his library – how that same father now, strangely enough, is extremely supportive of what I am and say and do. Not only supportive, but proud as well. And appreciative. And enthusiastic. And admiring.

Surviving war is an excellent training process. If it weren't so brutal, I'd recommend it as an excellent start-up course in life. I feel that over years of endurance, hard work and perseverance, of determination and conviction, of claiming our right to stay alive, to be free and to be ourselves, of fighting the biggest wars as much as the smaller ones, our will can indeed move mountains for us.

In my case: will and poetry.
     And poetry is definitely another story.

III

# An Arab Woman
# Writing Erotic Poetry

A better world is not possible without freeing the minds,
bodies and most of all language of women.
*Nawal El Saadawi*
Egyptian writer, activist and psychiatrist (1931–)

The first time I used the word penis in a poem, I must
have been twenty-five or twenty-six years old. My father
read it (he and my mother were, and still are, my number
one readers and fans), and could not help being horrified.
'How can you write such an atrocity, and publish it under
your own name?' he protested. His voice was somewhere
between disbelief and indignation. 'Couldn't you have used
the word "column" instead?'

'Well, Father,' I replied, 'to tell you the truth, I've had

enough of columns, pillars, pipes, spears, hoses, and all the infinite orchestra of phallic metaphors. I am writing a prose poem about a penis for a poetry magazine, and I'd like to name it.'

It was as simple (and as complicated) as that.

Needless to say, my dear dad hid the magazine away after publication, and prayed fervently that nobody from the family would see it and discover my scandalous hallucinations.

Why am I telling you this anecdote? Not because the penis is necessarily a wonderful writing topic, obviously. My main motive is to point out the stages of my progress from freedom of thought to freedom of expression. As you will notice, that progress did not occur quickly enough, despite the catalysing effect of the 'Marquis and Company', and my instinctive 'perverse' predispositions. While my subverted and subversive thoughts and fantasies ran freely, guiltlessly, scandalously, in my head, it took me quite a while to free my language from the fear of words. I started writing when I was eleven, and more than fifteen years had passed before I dared to express my real ideas and convictions in Arabic in a confident way. In fact, when now I read my poetry from the 'pre-penis' era, I feel angry, ashamed and nauseated, because that era reminds me of how women have been deprived of expressing their bodies for so long in our culture. I feel angry because of the malicious castration that has been unjustly carried out on the Arabic language, and, consequently, on my use of it. And ashamed, and nauseated, by the number of sugary terms and metaphors I used to employ in order to hide my real self. It is not a coincidence that my first book of poetry was in French. I started by cowardly hiding in French in order to avoid confronting Arabic.

You see, Arabic language takes pride in the richness of its allegories, symbols and synonyms. So why handle the risk of saying 'breast' when you can go on and on about hills or mountains (depending on the size of the bra), and apples or pears (depending on the shape of the protuberance)? Why hurt the sensitivity of the reader by mentioning the clitoris, when you can use your imagination to describe it as the 'flower of paradise' or the 'lip of heaven' or – if you are really talented –'volcano's doorknob'?

Don't get my sarcasm wrong: I love images. And they are part of the poetic game, of course. But I'm also convinced that this game lies elsewhere: in the strength of the message I'm sending. In the angle from which I'm sending it. And in the tension that it grasps and conveys.

That is what I discovered when, one day, I finally had the guts to say: enough. When I finally revolted against my spineless fear of Arabic words (as malicious as a cancer that eats you up in silence). When I finally asked myself: why should I agree to being treated as a minor? Who is to say what my limits as a writer are, if not myself? Which 'alien', external criteria will decide whether my employed dose of freedom is an 'overdose' or not? And at the peril of being labelled as impudent, insolent and provocative (which is exactly what happened later), I went on to write about desire, orgasms, hips, men, tongues, nipples and/or any body part or illicit idea I needed to refer to in my text.

And ever since that day, the body and eroticism have been my main inspiration.

'There is only one of two possible options: either the Word drains Eroticism, or Eroticism drains the Word' (Georges Bataille).

'Why Eroticism? Why the Body?' are questions that I am frequently asked. And my only answer to them is another question: do we writers really choose our topics, or do they choose us?

I am personally, and genuinely, convinced of the latter.

Why the Body, then? Simply because my body is an integral part of me, inseparable from my soul and my mind, and it is the temple of all my experiences and the terrain through which I live life. It is the Earth that welcomes into its womb the passions and the ideas, the sun and the moon, the fears and the dreams, the rain and the wind, the rivers and the birds and the people. Life, to me, is a physiological, physical, instinctual, sensory experience, in as much as it is also an emotional, psychological and intellectual one. And so is writing. To me, everything is palpable, and can be touched: words, thoughts, feelings, the unconscious, imagination, love, etc. If I write about the body and sex, about my desires and needs, I don't do that to titillate readers, as the machismo of some Arab critics accuses me of doing, but in order to be true to what I live inside, and what preoccupies me.

I do not separate the subject matter of my life from the subject matter of my writing: any experience that I live is a potential text (written, or yet to be written), and everything that I write is a potential life experience (lived, or yet to be lived). When I write, I feel like I am writing with my body and on my body, with my nails and from them, and that the words are erupting from my pores and being inscribed on my skin. It's a brutal, violent and bloody hunting trip, as much as it is a sensitive, contemplative journey. This is also how I read, and love: words and feelings echo in my flesh as hard as they do in my conscious and unconscious mind. In my daily life, my intimate spirit does not separate from my intimate body: each one is a side of the other, a twin, a partner in crime.

But the same question keeps popping up: 'Why the Body?'

'Why the hell not?' I retort. And why the need for explanations and justifications? I realise this polemic might seem pointless and superfluous, *dépassé* even, to many Westerners, since there are now in the West more than a thousand male and female authors exploring the erotic writing realm and processes, and to them such an exploration seems entirely matter-of-fact. But it is not this way, unfortunately, in the Arab world; a world where costly taxes are imposed on freedom of speech, especially that of women, and where many people still speak of the purity and virtue of literature, as if it had some moral mission!

If this claim were indeed true, what would we do with Céline, or Pound, or Genet? What would we do with Sade, and Nabokov, and Bataille, and Calaferte, and Nin, and Miller, and the hundreds, even thousands of writers who violated, and still violate, fortunately, rules and conventions of political correctness, without wavering one second? True candour is being honest with oneself and with the other, and I believe that writing about sex is completely natural, instinctual, normal and logical, to the extent that I loathe all questions or astonishment or curiosity (or condemnation, particularly and most of all) about the subject. On my brighter days, I try to be understanding, or forgiving, and rise above it, attributing this 'deviant' reaction to our sly Oriental society and its habit of sticking its head in the sand (we're a strange breed between peacocks and ostriches). But I confess that understanding, forgiving and rising above it are hard to do all the time, especially with a temperament like mine; even more so when it comes to dealing with the cowardice, disingenuousness and double standards of our jolly Arab world.

Some Arabs speak of the virtuous mission of literature, while denying writers freedom of expression. Is there a more whorish act than depriving an author of his/her words?

Let's call things by their names: censorship is an act of RAPE.

Which brings me to the necessity of detailing another pertinent fact: all the double standards, all the deprivation, frustration and boundaries that I, and many other Arab writers, have witnessed and keep on witnessing, apply to women, as I've mentioned above, much more tyrannically than they apply to men. In many cases, they do not even apply to men at all. For in our dear old Arab world, men are allowed to talk rather unreservedly about their genitalia (not to mention using them unreservedly as well). They are allowed to talk about woman's genitalia too, as a free bonus. As for the woman, she has to content herself with being the blessed 'receiver' of male words, the passive subject of the male texts. For she was not born to express. Rather to BE expressed. The French philosopher Michel Onfray wrote in his book, *Power of Existence*: 'When literature produces the counterpart of a woman Casanova, and when this name becomes a positive depiction of the person that it describes, then and only then can we speak of a real parity between men and women.' I don't believe that what Onfray meant in this statement was that women needed to live their sexuality in a banal way, the way poor Casanova did, in order for them to be equal with men. The solution is surely not for women to fall into the trap of quantity over quality. He was rather evidently talking about the different connotations that a description holds and conveys, only because of gender discrimination. And in that sense, his words apply perfectly in the Arab male (and often also female) critics' circles.

In fact, our critics generally use the word 'daring' to describe women writers exclusively: if a woman transgresses, she is 'daring'. If a man transgresses, this is ordinary because he is 'examining all aspects of life through his writing'. If a woman writes of sex among other things, she is predestined to be described as a daring 'erotic writer' (not that I'm particularly bothered by the label; rather, by the discriminative stigma it carries in our part of the world). If a man writes of the same subject, it is just a topic like any other, completely normal.

But these writings ARE indeed normal, whether written by a 'him' or a 'her'. And they should be out in the open. When are we in the Arab world going to stop discussing the body and sex either in painfully convoluted metaphors, or in terrible clichés? I am astounded, for example, by Arabic translations of Western movies. The passionate Julia Roberts and Richard Gere don't 'make love', but 'spend the night together'. And the beautiful Charlize Theron doesn't tell her girlfriend that she drowned her lover in kisses, but that she 'hung out' with him. As for that peeping tom Brad Pitt, he doesn't see Angelina Jolie nude, but rather '*au naturel*'. And let us not forget that Sophie Marceau does not have glorious breasts, but rather, geographical 'slopes'. In short: innumerable cowardly ways around the facts; a tragicomic rewriting of terms; and a pathetic dissociation of the translation from the original.

Consequently, my next question is at the heart of this book's subject matter. For asking: 'what does it mean to be an Arab woman?' means we must also ask: 'What does it mean to be a woman writer in an Arab country?'; and even more controversially: 'What does it mean to be a woman writer who writes without compromise in an Arab country?'

ॐ

To be a woman writer in an Arab country means, of course, suffering cultural 'blackouts' and underestimation, and being marginalised, whether innocently or systematically, by men or by women, or by both together.

To be a woman writer in an Arab country means to need to be rather cunning and slippery, to show a bit here and to mask a bit there.

To be a woman writer in an Arab country means, for many – but not for all, fortunately – to write things in code, so that, for example, a lover becomes a 'good friend', and a rapist father would be the father of 'the poor girl next door'.

To be a woman writer in an Arab country means to face, frequently, the insulting suspicion that a man in your shadow is writing what you are publishing under your own name.

To be a woman writer in an Arab country means to impose strict self-censorship, a thousand times harsher than any official censorship imposed from the outside.

To be a woman writer in an Arab country means to plan

meticulously and move astutely in the right social circles, preening and sweet-talking.

As for being a woman who writes without compromise in an Arab country, it means to be, on top of all the above, sassy and rude and brave. It means to be prepared for the 'scandal'.

It's not easy to be a woman who writes without compromise in an Arab country. It's not easy to take your clothes off, layer by layer, in front of strangers. It's not easy to expose others to your ideas, your life, your visions, your dreams, your fears, your inspirations, your mistakes, your failures and your confessions, when these others are not just readers, but ruthless 'judges' of you as a person. It's not easy to face up to the monster of prejudice and embarrassment, and to prove, despite that intimidating monster, your ability to express your ultimate self: your self in its strength as well as its weakness, in its disappointments and its hopes, in its beauty and its ugliness, in its heights and its depths, in its glittering nobility and its baseness.

No, it's definitely not easy to be a woman who writes without compromise in an Arab country. People know that very well. And this is why every woman writer is swamped by a slew of patriarchal accusations. How many times, for example, have steamy sex scenes in a novel penned by a woman become an excuse for denigration and rumour about that woman writer's sexual life and adventures?

∂♥

And this woman deserves to be noticed, heard and acknowledged, because it is not simple, or painless, being her. And there are indeed many of this calibre in our culture and language. That's why it is sad that the majority of Western interest in our writings, for example, is not well channelled, and prefers melodramatic, sensationalist or misguided texts, at the expense of real literature: a literature that can speak to the inner truth of the human being, wherever he or she is, because it is the holder of a universal truth.

It might seem that I am putting subversive/erotic literature above all other genres, and that is definitely not my aim. But a woman writing erotic/explicit literature in the Arab world is claiming freedom as a vital necessity, as opposed to many Arabs who view it as a luxury. Freedom as a necessity: the freedom to write unambiguously, as much as the freedom not to; the freedom to shock, as much as the freedom not to. In short: the right to CHOOSE. To decide for oneself what one wants to say, and live, and feel, and do. Nothing is more important on both the intellectual and personal levels. And that freedom is what poetry is all about.

ح

Talking about the relationship between poetry and freedom, and going beyond the debate concerning erotic writing, being a poet is quite complicated in itself, to say the least. We belong to an endangered species which is not best equipped for a risk-free life on planet Earth. And don't think I'm indulging myself in the 'you cannot write poetry if you don't have a miserable life' cliché. Quite the contrary. I'm a frustrated Epicurean poet who definitely wants to be happy. I just don't always know how. (By the way, do you? R.S.V.P!)

Having said that, to be an Arab poet is an almost impossible identity to hold. Why? Simply because, on top of the above-mentioned impediments, we are plagued by a catastrophic reading indicator. I'll let the numbers speak for themselves. According to recent statistics,[1] I live in a region where fewer than 0.1% of its 270 million people read; where merely 40% of that depressing 0.1% read books; and where 9% of the 40% of the initial 0.1% actually read poetry ...

You do the maths: that would leave us, according to my modest calculating skills, with 9,720 people reading poetry, in an immense Arab world that 'proudly' claims to have more than twenty thousand poets! Wouldn't you call that an irony? Well, you won't see any of us Arab poets laughing. So

---

1.  *The First Arab Report on Cultural Development*, published by the Arab Thought Foundation, Mu'assasat al-Fikr al-'Arabi, 2008, in Arabic.

where does that leave us? It precisely corrals us into a circle, a tiny stifling circle. Add to that the difficulty of finding a local publisher, spice it up with the hopelessness of ever being translated into another language, dip it in the condescension of people towards writers in general, and towards poets in particular, and you'll have yourself a perfect five-star poetic hell! So many days I wake up feeling my language strangled, hanging on a rope, useless ...

So why do I write poetry? Why don't I just write novels, like many people ask? Because 'poetry is proof that life is not enough,' as Fernando Pessoa once said. Because poetry is an URGENCY, an intense, passionate story without preliminaries, that suits my impatient soul. Because it is a never-ending swordfight between myself and me. Because it helps me realise I am alive. Because it is a multiplication of life. Because it is my flesh as I like it: without the protective skin.

Yet the gloomy facts are there:

'Every Arab reads a quarter of a page annually.'[1]

'Poetry merely represents 0.2% of the book market in Europe'[2]

---

1. *The First Arab Report on Cultural Development*, published by the Arab Thought Foundation, Mu'assasat al-Fikr al-'Arabi, 2008, in Arabic.
2. Sebastien Dubois, 'La poésie en Europe', 2003.

'It's mostly older people who read poetry.'[1]

These and other fatal comments keep on echoing ruthlessly in my head. But what are numbers for, anyway?

We don't write poetry to be hip. We don't write poetry to be recognised. And we certainly don't write poetry to be famous.

We write poetry to be free.

And that, for me, will always be the only, the crucial and the scariest reason of all.

'No matter how much progress has been made, there is still a world that for women is taboo. And in that world lies her freedom.' (Zaha Hadid). In fact, the first poem I ever wrote, aged twelve, was entitled 'Ma liberté'. Some would call this a coincidence. I prefer to call it destiny. And we all know that between coincidences and destinies, there lies a huge difference.

I have learned that difference while creating my magazine, *JASAD* ('Body' in Arabic).

But that, too, is a different story.

---

1.  http://www.guardian.co.uk/uk/2006/jan/29/poetry.books

# IV

# An Arab Woman
# Creating a Magazine about the Body

> I've never been myself
> I've never had a name
> But I ran to my body and I named it
> And from the border of perdition I cried:
> Save me oh my 'I'...
> *Maysoun Saqr Al Qasimi*
> Emirati poet (1959–)

Am I crazy?

I often ask myself that question, with all the rationality and irony that I am capable of. To be honest, the answer is that I might very well be: I'm not sure. I am not even sure if it is such a bad thing to be crazy, in the eccentric, daring, out-of-the-box sense of the word. What I am quite sure of, in return, is that I am obstinate, sometimes to an absurd (some might say stupid) extent. I have also trained myself to handle controversy, because of my writings and ideas. And even though I do not believe or appreciate the logic of 'I shock, therefore I exist,' and provocation and its side effects are not things that I particularly seek, I nonetheless feel capable of dealing with them, when necessary.

And it became more and more necessary after the birth of *JASAD*.

I had started thinking about setting up my own editorial business in 2006. Being a writer and a journalist, it soon became evident to me that I would like to establish a small publishing house, and begin by editing a cultural magazine. Not just any cultural magazine, though. I was in search of something different, strong and needed. And it wasn't long before the axis of the Body imposed itself, for two main reasons: firstly, the body is the universe inside which my own poetic language chose to express itself. It is both my passion and my tool. Secondly, I was feeling increasingly frustrated because our beautiful Arabic had been unfairly deprived of an important part of its potential vocabulary and imagination. Most themes relating to the body had become a taboo in our recent history, while our ancient literary heritage is loaded with works that would make even the most liberated Western writer blush. It was an absurdity, to say the least.

That is why I started, in the early days of 2007, conceiving *JASAD* magazine, from my small home office in Jounieh (a coastal city on the outskirts of Beirut), sitting tirelessly for hours and hours in front of my laptop. 'You must be out of your mind' was a sentence I soon got familiar with, because it was almost the only thing that I heard whenever I shared the idea of my project with a close friend or a family member. 'This is neither the place nor the moment,' they all told me repeatedly. Even the lawyer, whose task was to draw up the legal framework of my company and to get me the publication licence, was dreading the consequences of the enterprise. But my only thought was: 'Well, aren't we supposed to invent the right moment? What is our merit if we just wait for the right moment to come to us?'

That is why I wasn't shocked when, as soon as the founding of *JASAD* was reported by some of the Arab press in the fall of 2008, I faced some strange reactions, most of which came by email, some through press articles, but several via certain 'do-gooders', who passed on negative talk on the pretext of friendliness.

Let me introduce you at this point to the wide range of appellations and epithets that have been linked to my name because of *JASAD*: *immoral, dissolute, unethical, sinful, debauched, corrupt and corrupter, depraved, decadent, criminal, wicked, unscrupulous, dishonourable and devious.*

And then there were the poisonous, threatening phrases of the sort: *You deserve to be stoned to death. You will rot in Hell. You should be ashamed of yourself. How dare you? You are corrupting our kids. God will punish you. We spit in your face. We pray someone throws acid at you* ... (the latter, I admit, caused me terrifying nightmares for two consecutive weeks).

Had we been living in the era of witch hunts, I would have most certainly been strangled, stabbed, hanged, burned and drowned all together at the same time.

ﻦ

Yet, strangely enough, despite the frightening violence of some of the reactions, I have been invulnerable and perfectly immune to almost all these attacks.

I was immune for three reasons, the first two being personal, and the third one circumstantial.

The first reason for my immunity was that I'm the sort of person who refuses to be bullied. This might seem self-congratulatory, but I will say it anyway: I've discovered that my delicate skin, contrary to what it seems, can handle lynching and bruises. I don't mean to say that I'm invincible, or conceited, but rather that I am simply one of many women who enjoy going down difficult, untrampled paths, and into the open horizon, in life as well as literature, even if these choices cost a great deal.

The second reason that has kept me immune is that I have always despised unanimity; for me, unanimity means the herd mentality. The person who courts consensus has no colour, no taste, no smell. We shouldn't need an obsequious court to feel safe. We shouldn't need to please ALL the others to feel pleased about ourselves. Enemies are inevitable (some say necessary), and so be it. This does not necessarily mean we have to defy forcefully and gratuitously, because being different just to be different is silly folklore. Nor should we welcome hatred and envy for no reason. It means that we need to be multifaceted women, not photocopied from others; women with their own private opinions, their own thoughts, their own stands.

As for the third reason for my invulnerability, it is undoubtedly the support that I have enjoyed from two key persons who were in the government when *JASAD* was launched: Tarek Mitri, then minister of information, and Ziad Baroud, then minister of the interior; both esteemed intellectuals and cultured, open-minded human beings, who respect, and fight for, freedom of thought and expression. It was a happy coincidence that the magazine was born under such auspicious political conditions, in a country where mediocrity is the reigning trait of people in power. Both ministers, obviously, have received innumerable complaints, and faced pressure from both religious and non-religious figures and institutions to close down the magazine. But they have resisted. And for that – I mean for both of them doing the decent thing that every person in power *should* do – I owe them a huge debt of respect and gratitude. It isn't easy when you have to face daily Shiite radicals, Sunni radicals and the Church, to mention but a few pieces of our religious mosaic. So, in short, to both of them I say: *Bravo!*

'What I hide by my language my body utters,' wrote Roland Barthes in *A Lover's Discourse*. But there I was, uttering with my language what my body was told to hide, and immune to the hostile responses to *JASAD*. I wasn't surprised by them either, because this was exactly the kind of reaction I had expected to greet a publication concerned with the 'literatures, sciences and arts of the Body' in the Arab world. To make matters worse, the magazine is in Arabic. And as if that wasn't enough, the creator and editor in chief is a woman with a history of challenging a norm or two.

At this point, allow me to note that *JASAD* is not a pornographic magazine, as many Arabs have classified it. I am not the Hugh Hefner of the Arab world. Yet the magazine is not defending itself against the charge of being pornographic out of primness, or out of a puritanical mentality. Certainly not. In Lebanon, and in other Arab countries, we live with enough pornography of the political, social, artistic, cultural, mental, intellectual and moral variety, not to fear the least harmful type of all.

But *JASAD*'s key aim is not to help men ejaculate when masturbating, rather to inquire intellectually into the consciousness of the body, and into its unconsciousness. To do this by meditating, delving deep, experimenting, rebelling, being awake, sleeping, dreaming, having visions, hallucinating, writing, sculpting, drawing and dancing, thereby creating a cultural body for our Arab bodies.

So I did not expect an explosion of public applause for *JASAD*. On the other hand, I hugely appreciated the support and encouragement that was shown to me by many readers. I despise and criticise people who victimise themselves (one of the many less appealing human traits that Arabs seem to suffer in abundance), and I don't see myself as a victim. As much as I've been attacked and insulted, I've been praised and encouraged. Complaining is not an option.

Plus, I can't pretend I didn't see it coming. I certainly didn't imagine for one moment that the general public would seize upon and embrace the idea of this magazine. How could I expect that from our culture – or, should I say, from our varied and contradictory Arab cultures? Cultures which don't distinguish themselves, sadly, by anything other than the perpetuation and promotion of inferiority, hypocrisy, degradation ... and censorship.

Ah! The famous black angel looming over our Arab Bermuda Triangle of sex, religion and politics. Had it not been so vicious at times, I would almost have pitied it.

For what can censorship really hope to achieve, when banning a book guarantees it notoriety and widespread success?

Why impose censorship in an age when, at the press of a button, we can get all the information we need and more?

Censorship should be underhand and sly, but it is stupid beyond belief in our Arab world.

Censorship should be advanced, but it is primitive beyond belief in our Arab world.

Official Arab cultural institutions claim that censorship protects cultural values, but it only protects narrow cultures: the cultures of deceit, backward thinking and the Dark Ages. These institutions claim to be transparent and modern, but in reality they are covered in thick layers of dust: the dust of lies, falseness and regression.

It is the crisis of the Arab mind, official and institutional, and even the non-official and non-institutional one, that wants everything in the Arab world to be reactionary, infantile and obscurantist. It is the power of religion, the power of the state, the power of the society, the power of the tribe, the power of the family, the power of terror, and the power of taboos that takes hold of its victims.

The Arab mind is in crisis. And because of this, it wants everyone to be in crisis with it. It wants to reassure itself that no question will be asked to upset the status quo. The Arab mind cannot handle questions, because questions can hurt and upset the murky calm of the swamp.

Then we hear Arabs talking and complaining about the misunderstanding that the Other confronts us with, while they do nothing but make this misunderstanding worse, by giving it excuses and pretexts, provoking the West into making generalisations – sometimes racist ones – about Arab culture and civilisation.

'Censor the body and you censor breath and speech at the same time. Your body must be heard' (Hélène Cixous). How could we Arabs survive this scary world full of filthy temptations without censors to save us, I wonder? How could we be the saints that we all are, and the prophets that we all are, without their protecting Big Brother eyes? In fact, most people in our happy Arab countries are ethereal and unearthly: immaterial beings that, somehow, are born and grow up without bodies, without either sexual organs, needs, impulses, fantasies, vices or transgressions, and without secret naughty habits, or public ones either.

Most people in our happy Arab republics and kingdoms are zealous about something or other.

Come on; let's list these zealous factions, together:

There's the faction that defends conservatism and is fervent – in appearance only, yes, but with the height of all malice – about the concepts of chastity and purity. These people are zealous to preserve the hymens of the eye, the nose, the ear, the throat, of language, of the imagination and of dreams, and of anything else they can dream up to protect. These fragile and sensitive membranes apparently keep, all by themselves, our honour safe from the mire, from affront, from insult and from the threat of being torn by any kind of obscene penetration. But, like someone who sweeps dust under the carpet in order to feel secure and ends up believing the illusion of this fake cleanliness, these conservatives have fooled themselves into thinking that the illusion is the truth.

Then there is the faction of pessimists, symbolically known in Arabic as *ravens*. These particular zealots focus on any initiative that aims to refresh the stagnant waters of the quagmire, indulging their seemingly eternal need to sound the death knell before the initiative has even been born. Their flaccid philosophy is asserted by the incessant croaking of that same old refrain – 'It's all in vain, so why bother?'

Then there are the zealous saboteurs, with their biological instinct to put a spanner in the works. They make sure that anything that overcomes its paralysis and gets up and walks, without their blessings, trips over and falls back down again.

And last but certainly not least, there is the spiteful faction, whose adepts are as zealous as can be about their violent urge to spread poison. They do this under the pretence of a concern for *personal well-being*, and for *good reputation*, and on whatever other similarly believable pretexts they can find ...

Do you find my statements too theoretical? I will be more explicit and direct then. This is how most of us Arabs are, in short:

We applaud nudes by Robert Mapplethorpe, Man Ray and Spencer Tunick, but when similar erotic art by Arab artists is displayed in an Arab cultural magazine, we condescendingly call it pornography;

We exult in the greatness of Henry Miller, Anaïs Nin and Vladimir Nabokov, to name but a few, as examples of writers who broke taboos with real flair. We applaud them to such an extent that it's almost impossible to find an interview with an Arab writer who doesn't mention one of them, praise them, and brandish their name as a 'crucial literary influence'. But when an Arab cultural magazine publishes poems, stories and texts by Arab writers belonging to the genre of literary eroticism, we call it decadence;

We celebrate, with the height of ceremony, the genius of Picasso, Balthus and Courbet, and their forebears and descendants. But, on the other hand, similar paintings by Arab artists, shown in an Arab cultural magazine, are reviled for their corrupt moral values;

We shout 'Bravo!' at the Japanese film director Nagashi Oshima (*In the Realm of the Senses*), the Italian Bernardo Bertolucci (*Last Tango in Paris*), and the Polish-American-French Roman Polanski (*Bitter Moon*) and at other foreign filmmakers who have violated the forbidden, and continue to do so, with great courage and artistry. But we call the discussion of these kind of films in an Arab cultural magazine, depravity.

And so on, and so forth. Talking about excision and circumcision is taboo. Talking about gay life? Taboo. About dangerous self-mutilation rituals? Taboo. About how psychological complexes affect gender identity? Taboo. About the relationship between the body's social dimension and the eye? Taboo. About fetishistic practices? Taboo. About our subjective experience of our reflection in the mirror? Taboo. About the question of sexual identity? Taboo. About contemporary novels' critical perspectives on sex? Taboo. About the visions of desire? Taboo. About the male body, caught between being concealed and being absent? Taboo. About orgasmic moments in Sufi practice? Taboo.

This is how most of us Arabs are: 'We want something and we spit on it,' as the famous Lebanese saying goes. We constantly and obsessively think about sex, but dare not talk about it. We rid ourselves of one so-called abomination with one hand, then practise intellectual debauchery, which is much worse, with the other. One unified schizophrenic Arab nation, the vast majority of which stands united behind a constitution of ignorance, hypocrisy, backwardness, malice, lies, and the art of hiding behind a ridiculous and scanty screen.

ﻊ

Needless to say, I not only felt angry because of these reactions, I also felt insulted, and ashamed; ashamed of my
country and culture, or rather, to be accurate and just, of
what they have become, under the mischievous spell of
religious extremism and obscurantist/repressive political
regimes; ashamed that I, being an intellectual living here,
in this hopeless place at this hopeless period of our history,
was submitting myself to this humiliation, and accepting
these daily doses of threats and constraints to my freedom
of expression; and ashamed of our hypocrisies and double
standards, which are forcing me and many others to fight
for what should be our simple rights as human beings.

Some friends say to me: 'Consider yourself lucky. You
should be grateful that your magazine hasn't been censored
or banned yet.' Grateful?! Why should I be grateful for what
is duly mine? Why should I thank anybody for granting
me what I need to take for granted? Who are these people
to decide what we can or can't say, what we can print or
can't print, what we can or can't show? Who and what gave
them the right to choose on our behalf? If they don't like
the magazine, they simply need not buy it. I respect their
right to refuse it, but I demand equal respect for my right
to produce it. It is not an exaggeration to say that these
boundaries make me feel loathed and treated with a lethal

condescension. And let us not forget that Lebanon is light years ahead of other Arab countries.

"When one doesn't name the illness, one cannot heal it" (Etel Adnan). Frequently I wonder, by persevering in naming the illness, like many others are doing, and by insisting on staying here, on not leaving this hypocritical region to live elsewhere (and the temptation to leave has been, and still is, very strong at times), am I challenging or surrendering? Am I a dissident or an accomplice? How different would things have been if I weren't a woman? And, most importantly, what does being a woman really entail?

The question is tricky. And the answer is, of course, another story.

V

# An Arab Woman
# Redefining Her Womanhood

No change in the everlasting power hierarchy, and no fighting
against the demonisation of women and their exclusion from
the work, education and struggle camps are possible, without her
entering all active fields with the will of her individual choice.

*Khalida Said*
Syrian academic, critic and intellectual (1932–)

Let me grab the bull by the horns right from the start:

I definitely am what you would call a woman 'with balls',
but I don't have any penis envy;

I am a highly paid career woman, but I hate having to pay
the restaurant bill when a man takes me out on a date;

I am an emancipated workaholic woman, but a massage
and a facial give me as much pleasure and fulfilment as a
successful job-related project;

I am an intellectual woman, but I worry about my wrinkles and body weight as much as I worry about not having yet read the last Kundera;

I am not superficial, but a woman's oily hair, messy clothes and hairy armpits are on my scale as much a 'no-no' as silicon lips/cheeks/tits, and wherever else they inject that substance nowadays;

I am not superficial, but a man's dirty nails, bad breath and wrinkled shirt are on my scale as much a turn-off as a low IQ, lack of a sense of humour, and the tragic tendency for showing off;

I am an initiative-taking woman, but I lose my 'erection' in front of a spineless, gutless man as quickly (and irrevocably) as I lose it in front of a Neanderthal who thinks that visible chest hair, shiny fast cars and behaving like a jerk are indisputable proofs of his masculinity.

In short, I am what you would call a fanatic of femininity. And what does femininity mean? It is, of course, a complicated question. But to explain it bluntly, and visually, if I were to pick one example that most simply, yet effectively explains my view on femininity, I would pick the store front of the Sonia Rykiel boutique in the St. Germain neighbourhood in Paris: extremely beautiful, stylish and seductive dresses can be seen side-by-side with selections of books and new releases by novelists, thinkers, poets and philosophers.

Fashion and culture: food for the body, and food for the mind. External beauty and internal beauty, completing, and enriching, each other.

No one is shocked by this primal association between grooming the exterior and grooming the interior as much as we Arabs are. Why? Because, according to our intellectuals, the person who takes care of his/her outside is automatically shallow. And those who care about culture are supposed to be automatically neglectful of their external appearance. They should not have the time to care for 'trivial' matters such as hygiene, skin care and proper clothing, all concerned as they are with the serious existentialist, metaphysical questions of being.

The idea of two camps, the camp of the beautiful on one side, and the camp of the intelligent on the other, is a trap, and a persisting one, in spite of all the living counter-arguments that are out there nowadays. We should demand books, even in clothing stores. We should demand elegance, even in bookshops.

Here is a necessity, and there is a necessity. Here is need, and there is need. Here is hunger, and there is hunger. Here

is pleasure, and there is pleasure. Especially when it comes
to women.

Is there anything more magnificent than a woman
insisting on winning her battles whilst remaining a
woman?

Personally, I don't think there is.

In fact, the worst thing that can happen to a woman, in
the midst of the struggle that she is waging for her rights, in
order to gain respect, and to prove her ability to undertake
any job and find a place for herself in society – particularly
in Third-World societies – is for her to forget that she is a
woman; to lose the woman inside her.

Why do I say this, and what does a woman being a
woman mean?

I say this because some Arab (and non-Arab) women
believe that this battle for equality demands giving up
their femininity. But I don't need to look like a man to be
a strong woman. And I don't need to be against men to be
pro-women.

Furthermore: isn't the defeminization of women an act
of surrendering *par excellence* to men's blackmail and their
shallow view of the female entity as a sum of thighs, tits,
asses, lips, and so on and so forth?

Again: what does it mean for a woman to be a woman?
It does not mean of course the banality of wearing skirts,

putting on makeup, and growing long hair. It does not mean transforming her body into a piece of meat. In fact, and despite my firm belief that each person is free to do whatever he/she deems suitable with his/her body, I find the 'piece of meat' female prototype as humiliating and as degrading as the veiled one. Both annul the woman's genuine entity, which goes beyond treating her body as merchandise, or as a temptation to wipe her away with a black eraser.

Thus, a woman being a woman means for her to be, and to want to be, herself, and not anyone else's self. And especially not the man's self: the man-father's self, the man-husband's, the man-lover's, the man-brother's or man-son's.

It means that a woman must sustain this SELF, her personal self, with her guts, and her unconscious, and her body and her mind, fearlessly, without panic, or wariness, or taboo, or shame, or any other internal or social obstacles, whether visible or not.

It means that she sustains all this without worrying whether a man will approve of her, and her success, or judge her failure.

It means that she takes, instead of waiting to be given.

For a woman is her own sole expert, and her own guide to herself. She is the only reference on her body, and her spirit, and her essence. Neither the religious radicals who want her

absent should have a say on this, nor the superficially radical
who want to turn her into an object in a store window.

I as a woman need the man. No question about that.
And I love that need, and accept it, and nurture it, and
take my pride in it. I as a woman am aware that the man
needs me too. And I love that need, and accept it, and
nurture it, and take my pride in it as well. But there is a huge
difference between needing the other, and depending on
the other, becoming a mere appendage and an accessory of
his/hers. The first attitude is based on faith in oneself and
in the relationship, while the second is only built on low
self-esteem. In my modest view of the world, both human
identities go together, hand in hand, accomplices and equal,
challenging, motivating and supporting each other, yet
staying amazingly DIFFERENT. And if the woman has
to become equal to something or someone, then it is to
her own entity and identity, and to this entity and identity
alone. Then, she will be equal with her essential feminine
being, a being in continuous transformation. Beneath this
continuous movement, above it, outside of it, lies the void:
'Life is a process of becoming, a combination of states we
have to go through. Where people fail is that they wish
to elect a state and remain in it. This is a kind of death'
(Anaïs Nin).

๛

In this context, I remember very well my reaction when I once saw a picture of the Spanish minister of defence, Carmen Chacón, checking on her troops in southern Lebanon, in the spring of 2008, when she was seven months' pregnant. I've rarely seen anything as beautiful and as powerful as that sight: a young, pregnant, attractive woman checking on 'her' troops with all the might of her womanhood. A sight that condenses, in one expressive shot, the essence of my belief: the strength of femininity. The power of Lilith. Lilith, the original woman, the one who existed long before Eve, created from earth just like Adam. Lilith, the independent, free-spirited woman who refused to obey the man blindly, and left paradise of her own choice. Lilith, the rebellious woman, of whom Eve, created from Adam's rib, is nothing but a pale copy.

Obviously, the above anecdote about Chacón does not mean that I am blindly supportive of women in politics. Quite the contrary.

Women often ask me questions of the sort, "You must certainly have supported Ségolène Royale and Hillary Clinton in their respective bids for the presidency, right?" And when I reply 'No,' the woman asking such a question is taken aback. 'But how can that be? How can you not support them?'

Let me explain: the person asking the question is not

necessarily concerned with French or American policy and their ramifications for the situation in Lebanon. She is appalled at my answer for one reason only, which is that Ségolène Royale, just like Hillary Clinton, is a woman. And in her opinion, it is enough for a candidate to be a woman for that to be a reason for other women to encourage and support her. For me, traitor to my gender that I am, the fact that she has a vagina is not a sign of a candidate's qualifications, and I have not yet learned (nor will I ever learn) the secrets of blind allegiance to women's issues.

Of course, I would have liked Ségolène Royale, she of the graceful bearing and humanist discourse, to be elected French president. And I would have liked Hillary Clinton, she of the sharp intelligence and iron will, to make it to the top of American government. For no other reason than to exact 'revenge' for every woman who made it to politics at the expense of her femininity; or, the other way around, with no qualifications except her looks. But a presidential appointment, in my personal opinion, requires stronger experience and more depth than either Royale or Clinton possessed, for reasons that have nothing to do with them being female. So should I have supported them symbolically, just because all three of us wear bras before leaving the house in the morning?

No, and a thousand nos for such an insulting, superficial kind of solidarity. Women deserve more. Much more.

ه‍

On the subject of female solidarity, let me just mention this 'tragic' piece of news: recently, in Lebanon, a female-only taxi service was established for women who don't want to mingle with men; and many of the so-called fairer sex are exultant at the news, whooping and celebrating with a, 'It's pink! And so cute! And a woman is driving the cab – how original!

But this girls'-taxi, with its sickening lollipop colour, is a source of embarrassment for me as a Lebanese woman. And as an Arab woman. And as a woman in general.

Since when is a taxicab the site of 'dangerous liaisons'? Since when did we in Lebanon go back to conforming to the segregation of the sexes? We've only recently got rid of separate girls' and boys' schools, and other practices that produce inhibited men and women, knotted up in complexes, repression, ignorance and fear of the other sex.

In the recent past, we witnessed the Barbie generation (and we haven't outlived it yet); now, we are apparently witnessing the segregating girls'-taxi generation. These two examples might seem disconnected, but they are, in fact, quite similar. It's enough that each, in its own way, represents a conditioned mode of behaviour in the Arab world that has annoyed me since my youth: a categorising behaviour that separates the male from the female, and puts each of them in a different setting. As soon as a girl is born, her parents and relatives surround her with dolls of all shapes and sizes. One to spend the day with, one to hug at night, a third to drink tea with, a fourth to plan a wedding for. (*What is a little Arab girl without the perfect wedding plan? What meaning to her life if it is devoid of such a perspective?*)

On the other hand, when a boy is born, he is surrounded with ostensibly male toys: cars of all shapes and sizes, plastic soldiers and tanks and swords and guns. Even today, few parents rebel against this cliché, and avoid the pitfall. Wherever we go, girls wear pink and boys wear blue. She is supposed to be soft, peaceful, wistful and obedient (most of all obedient), and he is expected to be rough-and-tumble, down to earth, and a rebel.

Personally, I hated dolls. Not a single one – not Barbie, nor any of her sisters – managed to seduce me. I did not fall once – even before I knew enough to make a conscious decision – into the trap of archetypal femininity, the one which society imposes, and that limits our personalities, behaviours and thoughts.

I am a woman, yes. A woman of course. Proudly.

Absolutely. And very much so. But for God's sake, get that pink colour and all the clichés attached to it away from my sight. I remember one day that I clashed with my uncle, because he had dared to buy me a miniature kitchen, complete with a washing machine and an iron, for my birthday. I felt insulted that day, despite being just eight years old. Not because I despise cooking and washing and ironing and house chores in general. Quite the opposite, I feel a great deal of respect and appreciation for women who devote their time to caring for their families this way (and my mother is one of those, and I owe her a lot on that level). Plus, I do not consider the career woman the only model of successful, emancipated and efficient woman. But I am talking about choice, and in that choice lies all the difference between a subjugated and a free woman. I am all for a woman cooking if cooking is her wish and decision. I am against a woman cooking if cooking is expected of her, and imposed on her, for the sole reason that she is a woman.

My uncle unconsciously wanted me that day to conform to a female stereotype dictated by patriarchal society: the female stereotype of a woman who is only expected to cook and clean and wash and iron ... and who is waiting for the man to come home from work, from war, from politics, from thinking, and from the other estates of outside life.

I don't mean to put all the responsibility on men's shoulders. We do share a big part of that responsibility as well. We simply shouldn't accept being women 'who wait': whether it is an occasion, an opportunity, an event, or, obviously, a man. We need to get up, walk on, reach out for what we want and take it.

Or, at least, try to.

'I do not fight against men, but against the system that is sexist' (Elfriede Jelinek). I remember that, around fifteen years ago, when the famous John Gray book *Men are from Mars, Women are from Venus* came out, it was enormously successful on the popular level, not only in his native America, but also around the world, including the Arab countries, where many considered it to be the holy grail of relationships between men and women, and the absolute solution to all bonding problems, whether marital or otherwise. I confess that, despite being in my early twenties at the time, I read this alleged guide to 'improving communication between the sexes' with a sarcastic smile on my face, especially regarding the supposedly miraculous solutions proposed, whose dangerous simplicity was only outdone by the unoriginality of their clichés.

At that time I thought that nothing would surpass this

work's naïve depiction of the relationship between the sexes, with its prejudices and its lame pre-packaged answers and silly, 'well-meaning' advice. Then I read a book called *Are Men Necessary?* by the American writer Maureen Dowd, the *New York Times* columnist, and I knew that I had lost my bet against myself. For as much as Gray's book contains laughable generalisations about dealing with the 'historical misunderstanding' between men and women (a theory as simplistic as Samuel Huntington's 'clash of civilisations', albeit on a different level and subject), Dowd's book contains even more superficial slogans and propagandistic examples. Once the reader has sorted through the claustrophobic content, he or she is invariably led to the conclusion that she does not aim to champion the women's cause, as much as she aims to destroy men through deliberate provocation and brainwashing.

"Are men necessary?" Maureen Dowd asks. "Of course not!" answers, in ecstasy, an Arab female journalist who reviewed the book at the time, proving her assertion with the news that a group of American scientists had succeeded in creating artificial sperm extracted from a woman's bone marrow. Thus, a woman can from now on be self-sufficient enough to bear children without male 'interference'.

My astute colleague was applauding this invention in her

article, lauding it as a "revenge for women, for all the oppression and hardship they have borne". But the dear journalist failed to realise that a woman's need for a man is not reduced to his fertilising sperm. She failed to realise that neither she, nor many of the Arab women who rush to blame men for all their problems, admit that the oppression and hardship a woman faces are sometimes her own responsibility as well, because she surrenders and does almost nothing to change the dark situation she finds herself in; instead, she is content merely to complain about it.

Of course, I am not generalising, nor being cruel, insensitive and unfair to my sex. I know perfectly well how many horrors are perpetrated daily on women in some radical parts of the Arab-Muslim world. The most horrific of these practices in my opinion is what they dare to call 'honour killings'; for a woman irrevocably tarnishes her family's honour by engaging in pre-marital sex, or by getting herself raped, or if she seeks divorce, or when she elopes and marries against her family's wishes. Men 'responsible' for her consequently become victims, because their honour has been violated, so killing her is considered self-defence. One of many examples is Kifaya Husain, a sixteen-year-old Jordanian girl, who was lashed to a chair on 31 May 1994 by her thirty-two-year-old brother, before he slashed her throat. Her crime? She was raped by her other brother.

And let's not talk about female genital mutilation and its wicked aim of depriving women of their right to pleasure. Nor of prearranged marriages of little girls who can barely play house. The list of horrors and injustices is too long.

Notwithstanding that, it still annoys me that many Arab women's only response to their suffering is to complain about it instead of trying to find a solution, a window of hope, however small, somewhere in their daily reality. 'Where there's a will there's a way' is much more than a nice set of words.

ॐ

Plus, who said that men are women's worst enemy? I've met women who hate women, ally against them and fight them harder than any man would – mothers who remain silent in front of a rapist father; who are eager to find husbands for their thirteen-year-old daughters; who leave them without a proper education because 'they are predestined for marriage anyway, so why bother?'; who raise their sons to be even more discriminative and disrespectful towards women than their fathers.

I'm not in the habit of issuing blanket demographic claims about men and women; it's a practice I reject, and a naïve act that I am not convinced of at all. But there is a difference that few people recognise between necessary self-criticism and pathological self-loathing. Why should one woman be either the predestined enemy of men, or a blind ally of women, for the wrong, unconvincing reasons? For this I allow myself, at a distance from hysterical man haters, as well as from the large number of apathetic or voluntarily submissive women, to repeat several basic rights that are frequently ignored:

The woman's right to be for strong, intelligent and independent femininity, against aggressive slogans;

The woman's right to have non-belligerent relations with men, without these relations being interpreted as submissive;

The woman's right to be a man's equal without being tempted by a discourse of hegemony over him or one of similarity with him;

The woman's right to enjoy a bouquet of roses even if she drives tractors and changes engine oil;

Also, and especially, the woman's right not to blindly follow the crowd, and to believe in her choices, in her small battles, in the importance of cultivating her own private garden.

"We need to be assertive in our choices and desires in order to exist. Middle grounds lead to self-destruction" (Djamilah

Bouhired). To go back to the beginning: women's equality with men should be an assertion, outside the ring of demand and negotiation. In fact, it is often women's demands for equality that deprive them of it. The one making a demand puts herself in a position of weakness. She is the asker, and the other is the grantor. Let us instead consider this equality as basic, and behave as if it is a given fact (and it really is so). I am aware this is not always applicable, especially when discriminative legal frameworks are involved, but it can be applicable in many tiny details of daily life. And these CAN make a difference. In the long run, they can even influence laws and constitutions.

What is required, in the Arab world particularly, is for the woman to go far in crystallising her life one minuscule step after the other, without expecting anything from anyone, and without being a mirror reflecting what others think her image should be. The true issue is for her to regain her stolen, confused identity. Regaining this unknown, kidnapped identity, this compromised being that has been distorted under various forms of fear, conditioning and frustration, is the hardest battle that a woman must fight, and win.

As for the insultingly easy gains that are given to women as consolation prizes or as anaesthesia or bribes, these are landmines concealing treacherous compromises; so, we'd better not accept them.

Either everything. Or nothing. We need to win (or lose, evidently) our battles as ourselves, without conditions, alterations, deals or compromises to our womanhood. This is, in my opinion, the new Arab Femininity, and even the new Universal Femininity, that we need today. A femininity unafraid of its truth. Unafraid of its strength. Unafraid of its fragility. Unafraid of its greed. Unafraid of its weakness. Unafraid of its fierceness. Unafraid of its softness. Unafraid of its losses. Unafraid of its curiosity. Unafraid of its honesty. Unafraid of its madness. Unafraid of its mistakes. Unafraid of its talents. Unafraid of its beauty. Unafraid of its language. Unafraid of its power. Unafraid of its extremes. Unafraid of its experimentations. Unafraid of its contradictions. Unafraid of its youth. Unafraid of its maturity.

A femininity, in short, unafraid of its femininity.

I surely don't claim to be an example to be followed. I don't claim to be the precursor of anything. And I don't claim to have the answers: not at all. Quite the contrary: I am nothing but my failures, my errors, my questions, my doubts ... and my dreams.

And talking of doubts, now the moment has come for me to tell you a new story. My story with a multi-headed, omnipotent, alarming dragon.

He commonly goes by a weird name:

'God.'

VI

# An Arab Woman
# Unafraid of Provoking Allah

I shall stop claiming the rights of Saudi women when I start
seeing adult Saudi men being dragged to police stations if they
dare to drive their cars, and when the Saudi woman begins
wearing comfortable garments, while the Saudi man is forced
to wear a black veil, black gloves and black clothing, turning
him into an absent mass, and when he is told he has only two
places fit for him in this world: the house and the grave.

*Wajeha al Huwaider*
Saudi writer and human rights activist (1957–)

'Had you been a Muslim woman, you'd never have been
able to write what you write.'

"Had you been a Muslim woman, you'd never have
launched a confrontational project like *JASAD* magazine."

"Had you been a Muslim woman, you'd never say what you say, live the way you live, be who you are."

To all the sceptical, judgemental, prejudiced Western minds that keep making such hasty statements to my ears, I reply: you must have gone to a nuns' school for fourteen years before you can allow yourself to express such (erroneous) assertions. You must have had Arab conservative, Christian parents, and lived in an Arab conservative Christian mini-society, before you can allow yourself to utter such (biased) opinions. You must have experienced the Church's discrimination against the female gender, and witnessed from a close distance Christian fundamentalism, which is not so much better than Muslim fundamentalism, and read Saint Paul's words about women, before you can allow yourself to make such (invalid) declarations.

'Let the woman learn in silence, with all subjection. But I suffer not a woman to teach, or to use authority over the man: but to be in silence. For Adam was first formed; then Eve. And Adam was not seduced; but the woman being seduced, was in the transgression. Yet she shall be saved through childbearing; if she continues in faith, and love, and sanctification, with sobriety' (St Paul's first letter to Timothy, 2:11–15).

So is there really a difference between being a Muslim and a Christian woman in the Arab world today?

Is it truly 'easier'?

Is it accurate (and fair) to assume that Christianity is all about love and forgiveness and embracing the other, and Islam is all about bigotry and evil and killing innocent people?

Not if you're blindly pious. Not if you're vehemently anti-secular. Not if you abide literally by your religion's rules, whatever that religion is, and surrender your own judgment to a supposedly 'higher' one, and naïvely believe every single word your religious figures tell you, and adapt your life, and visions, and actions, to the endless vicious circle of laws and recommendations (which frequently go to an absurd extent) that someone else has thought and conceived on your behalf, and decided should work for you, and will grant you an unconditional 'entry to paradise'.

'Is man one of God's blunders? Or is God one of man's blunders?' (Friedrich Nietzsche). This is how I have come to think of it: with all due respect to people who believe in fairy tales (and need them), what could paradise be other than a wonderful illusion invented by a few geniuses (sometimes they are called prophets, other times saints and mystics, depending on the cultural and social contexts) in order to control the masses, promising them in return a reward that they will never be able to grant? Or, at least, a reward with no guarantee of delivery? Can you imagine an easier, yet more Machiavellian trick pulled on millions and millions of minds, eager to be comforted in their fears and doubts and day-to-day challenges and crises? Do you really want to bet your life, and principles, and behaviour, and choices, on THAT? Wouldn't it be healthier, and more rewarding, to set for yourself an earthly life ethic and morality, based on decency, respect and universal humanistic values? Wouldn't it be healthier, and more rewarding, to decide for yourself what your mistakes are, and try to correct them?

Plus, if paradise did indeed exist, who'd want to go there, honestly?

A place where everything is PERFECT?

A place where a man and a woman were punished for picking an apple and having sex?

Really?!

Give me a break!

ॐ

Back to our topic: Muslims promote fanaticism?

Christians promote the feeling of guilt. Which is no better.

Muslims believe in jihad?

Christians believe in burning in hell. Which is no better.

Muslims think it is OK for a man to have four wives simultaneously?

Christians consider sex a sin, only tolerated to bear children. Which is no better.

Muslims don't separate between state and religion?

Christians separate the body from the soul. Which is no better.

Muslims condemn women showing their hair?

Christians condemn women having abortions. And asking for divorces. And taking birth control pills. Which is no better.

I do not wish to fall into the trap of generalisations, and I am certain that any comparison between two religions is obsolete and unsound. This is certainly not a defence of Islam, nor a prosecution of Christianity. You can never be free in both. I have seen the worst from both sides. I have respectable, wonderful friends, who think like I do, and others who don't, from both sides. So this reasoning is not about proving which religion is better, which is more tolerant, which is more open and modern and inspiring and liveable. It is, to me at least, about realising that all religions are bad (bad for your common sense, bad for your life style, bad for your ability to choose, even bad for your health!)

when you move them from the sphere of spiritual nourish-
ment, where they belong (for those who seek it that way)
of course), to the sphere of your private and public lives,
where they are bound to ruin every chance of freedom,
equilibrium and objective judgment you might have.

ॐ

Some people, though, especially nowadays, and especially
in the West, follow a rather different reasoning. One based
on facts and assumptions derived from them. And this is
how their reasoning works:

When American singer Madonna, in the controversial
video clip of her song 'Like a Prayer' (1989), kissed the
statue of a black Jesus, and danced sensually in front of
burning crosses, she was harshly criticised by the Vatican
and the Catholics, because that video was considered
'blasphemy';

But when Dutch film director Theo Van Gogh released
his film *Submission* (2004), which was critical of the
treatment of women in Islam, and where Quranic verses
were seen projected on women's naked bodies in Arabic, he
was assassinated by a Dutch Moroccan Muslim;

*The Da Vinci Code*, Gilbert and George, Damien Hirst,
and their violent provocations of Christianity?

Harshly criticised.

Salman Rushdie, Taslima Nasreen, Ayaan Hirsi Ali and their violent provocations of Islam?

Fatwas and death threats.

I hear those comparisons, I understand their logic, but I am not convinced that they constitute a proof that Christianity is more tolerant than Islam. That's merely a bluff. For I am persuaded that the Church has found more hypocritical methods to fight those who dare to challenge its authority.

'We have just enough religion to make us hate, but not enough to make us love one another' (Jonathan Swift). Taking into account the real, terrifying problems constituted by Islamic fanaticism and terrorism today, and the social and political complications caused by the high tide of Muslim immigration, maybe the time has arrived for the West to admit that in order to have, it needs to give. I personally was born and raised in a country that had people of almost all faiths – Sunnis, Shiites, Druzes, Catholics, Orthodox, etc: a country where eighteen different religious communities shared (in salutary indifference, at least until 1975) this microscopic geographic, political and social space. And I learned, at a very young age, not to parade my convictions as if they were absolute and definitive truths that apply to everybody. I also learned that we need to make a choice between the rejection of evident symbols (and thus eliminate them), and the respect of evident

symbols (and thus accept them ALL); and that freedom
of expression is different from the freedom to offend, and
that the 'politically correct' and 'decently correct' are not
the same thing.

In order to have, we need to give: so enough of religious
exhibitionism/voyeurism, in all its forms. Praying should
be like making love: a private matter. Everybody speaks of
sexual obscenity, but almost nobody speaks of religious
obscenity. Those who make love in public are sent to prison:
it is maintained that it constitutes an offence against public
decency. I dream of a secular, uncontaminated world, where
the same treatment is reserved to those who transform their
religious convictions into a carnival.

Nonetheless, it is true that the Arab Christians, or the
'Christians of the Orient', as they are frequently referred to,
are nowadays – unfairly – rarely noticed and acknowledged,
and that the expression 'the Arab world' has become synonymous to many, whether from the outside or the inside, with
'the Muslim world'. It is also true that the Arab Christians
have played an important part in the development of the
region, culturally, socially, economically, both in ancient
Arab history (their modernising role in the Umayyad and
Abbasid periods is one shining example of that role), and

in the recent one. It is indeed true that the Arab Christians have always constituted a key, necessary and vital ingredient in the complicated yet rich mosaic of the Arab world, offering the privilege of a somewhat different perspective. But this is no reason to glorify them and consider them the sole saviours and modernisers of the Arabs. This is no reason to think that every emancipated Arab woman you see on the streets of Beirut has to be Christian, and that every oppressed woman behind closed doors is Muslim. The veil, the burqa, and their likes are awful of course. That is my personal point of view and I have never hidden it. But do the veil and the burqa really weigh more than the Lebanese Church's discrimination against women in cases of divorce, to cite but one example? Do they really weigh more than the Church clerics being, as much as the Al-Azhar sheikhs and the Shiite ayatollahs, the ultimate decision makers in people's private and civil lives? Do they really weigh more than the predominant laws in the majority of Arab states, which consider the husband/father an absolute reference, and the wife/mother, merely an accessory? Are the Arab Christian women more liberated only because they can wear whatever they want to wear (in principle, but not always)? Is the Lebanese Christian woman more emancipated only because she can go out at night? Is that what true liberation and emancipation are about, or are they about ensuring that her rights as a mother, as a daughter, as a wife, as an

employee, as a human being, are respected, and about getting her protected by an impartial and equitable legal and
civil framework? Isn't she being distracted by a few meaning-
less pleasing carrots that the authorities, whether religious
and or/political (what's the difference in the Arab world,
after all?), are handing to her in order to sidetrack her from
the real meaning of freedom and emancipation?

Again, is there an authentic, significant, definitive difference
between the situation of the Muslim and the Christian Arab
woman? I am afraid there is not. Not if you go in deep. The
injustice, double standards and prejudices are just more
obvious and visible with the first one, that's all.

And the obvious is almost always a trap.

'I do not understand: I sent you to a religious school. Your
mother took you to mass every Sunday. You used to pray
before you went to bed. You were baptised and you had
your first communion. How could you have grown up to
be like this? Where did I go wrong?' That's a question my
dad sometimes asks me, with genuine indignation, despite
his definite pride in my few achievements so far; an indignation lightened by a joking, forgiving tone that means:
I respect that this is who you are, but sometimes I find it

hard to accept, and I can't help but feel responsible for an educational 'failure'.

I tell him: "Where you think you went right is exactly where you went wrong. I am the product of that stiff religious education you gave me. An education which is bound to breed two species of people: the one 'burdened with complexes', and the one 'addicted to transgression'. Normality has no place there."

We need to go back to before the 'going right' and 'going wrong' era. To the pre-religious institutions era, the pre-'think like I do' era, the 'we are right and they are wrong' era. Let us go back even further: to the pre-original sin era, and all the distorted literature and logic influenced by it.

Pre-Adam. Pre-Eve. Pre-angels. Pre-demons. Pre-righteous. Pre-sinful. Pre-commandments. Pre-castigations. Pre-blessed. Pre-condemned. Pre-God. Pre-Devil.

And then let us start it, and start US, all over again from there.

So, am I provoking dear old Allah?

Is he angry with me, and will he chastise me?

Will I be condemned to eternal damnation and denied the ultimate pleasures of Heaven?

So be it. I am ready to take that risk. For I don't want an Allah, should he exist, that I cannot challenge and provoke, the way his concept challenges me and provokes me.

And, most of all, I do not want to live my present life thinking of the afterlife. This is it for me, folks. This is all there is, these forty or fifty or maybe ninety years on this earth, with all the small joys and disappointments that come with them.

As for the errors I make, the only punishment I acknowledge for having made them is my awareness of those errors, and having to live with it: there is, there should be, no heavier penalty on a person's soul, mind and heart.

And the only reward I want for my 'good deeds', if and when I do any, is to know that I've done them without expecting anything in return: no pat on the back, no bravos, no Saint Peter handing me the keys of the blessed kingdom. I am convinced that no recompense is sweeter.

God, you retort? I want to try facing that dragon. As a writer. As a woman. As a human being. With the tools of the writer. With the tools of the woman. With the tools of the human being.

As for the people who tell me that, as an Arab woman, I should obey the male, cover my hair and go to confession and ask for redemption whenever I have sex with a man without being his wife and without wanting to bear his

child, I leave them to their ridiculous convictions: these
are, after all, their only consolations in life.

And their worst punishment.

ح

"When religion starts proposing a female counterpart
to God, then I shall have greater respect for it" (Huda
Shaarawi). What is the responsibility of the Arab woman
amidst this discussion? What is her responsibility towards
religion and religious interference in her life and the impedi-
ment of her free choice? It is, in my view at least, to refuse to
be brainwashed and misled by a bunch of people who want
to keep her at bay. It is to realise there has to be something
wrong with all these religions that are strictly represented
by male gods and male figures (popes, sheikhs, ayatollahs,
priests, prophets, etc). It is to believe in the power of a
secular civil society, and to contribute to promoting it.

It is, in short, for her to THINK FOR HERSELF.

For it is time – it has been for a while – for us women of
the Arab world to challenge the preset patterns of religion.
And of politics. And of sexuality. And of writing. And
of life. And facing that challenge is what makes all the
difference between a typical, and an atypical, Arab woman.
Between a woman submissive enough to surrender to her
'fate' and to the limits imposed on her, and a woman strong

enough to live, and to say no, even when living and saying no mean losing sometimes.

But that is yet another story.
    And it will be my last. (For now.)

# VII

# An Arab Woman
# Living and Saying No

> I never will stop being free.
> I will sing the desires of my spirit,
> even if you crush me in chains.
> My song will gush from the depths.
> *Fadwa Touqan*
> Palestinian poet (1917–2003)

"Welcome to Beirut's Rafic Hariri International Airport,"
says the hostess's monotonous voice over and over again. A
modern, spotless, organised, practical airport. That place,
that cold spacious impersonal place, has started to look a
lot like home to me, especially in the last two years, since
I've been travelling a lot lately. I already have my secret
spots in it, my own preferred seat in one of the cafeterias
(where coffee, by the way, costs seven dollars: a scandalous

rip-off), my ideal internet point, my special bookshop, my lucky moving stairs. I have my superstitious rituals (put on red underwear when travelling, and always go inside the airport from door number two, with right foot first), my routine (check-in, smile widely at airline agent so that he or she overlooks the extra weight, buy cigars, avoid at any cost the perfumes area, get *Science et Vie* magazine, then sit down in self-service restaurant) and my culinary habits (cappuccino – no sugar; muffin – without chocolate chips; water – not sparkling). Many of the employees there are even starting to recognise me: when more than five Duty Free sales people start calling you by your name, you need to begin worrying about your life style. One of the officers at the customs asks me every single time he inspects my passport: "Don't you ever get tired of all this travelling?"

Don't I ever get tired of all this travelling? Well, I do, Mr Customs Officer. Of course I do. Often I get tired, worn out, fed up and torn apart. Often I feel estranged and confused, especially when I wake up in an unfriendly hotel room and it takes me a few seconds to remember exactly where I am; or when I see my face in a new mirror every morning, and hardly recognise it; or when I miss my two kids and curse the phone because it is never enough, never like the real thing. And let's not forget the unavoidable BEFORE and AFTER paramilitary procedure: pack the suitcase, close the suitcase, carry the suitcase, check in the suitcase, check out the suitcase (if you're fortunate and NOT travelling Alitalia), open the suitcase, empty the suitcase ... Over and over again, like a dull mantra. Like an exile in sequences. Or even better: like an exercise of exile that you need to repeat in order to master it.

And then, there is also, of course, the solitude that comes with being a vagrant soul in constant search of the big unknown. Not solitude in its antisocial meaning: quite the contrary, I am rather a sociable person and I love other people's company when it is interesting, clinically tested, taken in small doses, and not imposed on me. But I am talking about solitude as an internal psychological and intellectual condition: the one that allows you to listen to yourself, and thus to realise how helpless you are; to understand your brain and the world better, and thus to have fewer illusions about both of them; to feel weightless and open to all possibilities, and thus to easily sacrifice whatever you've built on firm land; to 'really' see things around you, away from any interruption, influence or distraction, and thus to be 'really' disappointed.

Disappointed then. Often exhausted. Bored as well from time to time. And certainly puzzled by all the different skies, faces, rhythms, noises, words, behaviours and pillows.

So why do I travel so frequently, I ask myself, if there is so much to moan about? Why all the trouble?

The answer is easy, really. Because travelling is living; and it is consequently worth all the trouble. Seeing the world and meeting people and discovering cultures is worth all the fatigue, all the mess, all the risks, all the perplexity and chaos and disappointment that come with the territory. This is one of the main purposes of existence. Watch new things. Read new things. Discover new things. Communicate new things. Feel new things. Learn new things. Love new things (and people, of course).

  If this isn't living, then what is?

But living is also about being proud of who we are.

  When I was a little girl, I used to say to everybody who would listen to me that I would have preferred to be a boy. I did not discover the extent of my foolishness until I experienced the wonder of being who I AM; the wonder of my hand. Of the old and fresh blood in my hand. The wonder of my wounds, wide open like frightening eyes; the wonder of the shores I would have to reach; of the circles I'd need to break to recreate my way; of the impossible identities and truths I would need to name; of the multiple images I would have to be, then un-be; of the man I would need to discover and love and receive and illuminate and liberate, but not replace; the wonder of life, of all the lives I would have to live despite life ...

That is, the wonder of being a woman. A real woman. And being proud of it.

'The woman is no victim of a mysterious fate: she should by no means assume that her ovaries condemn her to live eternally down on her knees' (Simone de Beauvoir). The time has come for woman to LIVE instead of just enduring life, and to free herself from the victim image. For she is not a victim, and should stop seeing and reflecting herself as a victim. She needs to accept and love herself. Who said being narcissistic is such a bad thing? Not when it allows you to embrace your truth and celebrate it. Not when it doesn't turn you into an insensitive, cruel, egocentric human being.

Women also need to free the man from his fear of the strong female: he should start considering her as a powerful, necessary, useful ally, not as a castrating menace hanging over his balls. Achieving that needs a lot of work from him, but also a lot of work from the woman herself: she should not use her strength to intimidate him, however tempting that might be.

So living is about accepting who we are. But it is about accepting change as well. This is one of the reasons why I always try to state my points of view while allowing myself some self-criticism, and a margin of variation. It is our human right to change. This is not synonymous with lacking consistency, as some rigid people like to think. Quite the contrary: it is about letting the universe get through to us and make its waves in our minds and souls. I don't want to be exactly the same in ten years, nor in five, nor in one for that matter. Don't stiff, inflexible people get bored with themselves? Don't they have enough of repeating the same words and ideas and concepts? I don't mean we should be moody and unstable; and I am certainly not in favour of unsteady and unreliable behaviour. I'm just saying: let's loosen up and not take ourselves too seriously. Let's always be open to other possibilities. Let's allow ourselves to be swept off our feet by new things. For becoming blasé is the worst thing that could ever happen to a human being. "Been there, done that." So sad ... it is the anti-living *par excellence*.

Living, last but not least, is also about losing. At least for me it is. For I am no superwoman. Far from it. And I've had my share of defeats and failures along the way:

Many times in my life I've been cowardly. And so I lost the battle;

Many times I've been stupid and narrow-minded. And I lost the debate;

Many times I've been over-competitive. And I lost the pleasure of competing;

Many times I've been arrogant. And I lost the privilege of being humble;

Many times I've been gratuitously authoritarian. And I lost the privilege of being fair;

Many times I've been evasive. And I lost my self-confidence;

Many times I've been unfocused. And I lost the target;

Many times I've done things only to prove that I can do them. And I lost the feeling of fulfilment;

Many times I thought I could easily outsmart my adversaries. And I lost to them;

Many times I was doubtful of my friends. And I've lost real friends;

Many times I've been trusting of the unworthy. And I got stabbed in the back;

Many times I imagined I was invulnerable. And I got badly hurt;

Many times I've been uselessly confrontational. And I got slapped in the face;

Many times I've said no, when I really wanted to say yes. And I lost a life-changing yes;

Many times I've said yes, when I really wanted to say no. And I lost a necessary no;

Many times I chose self-control over self-abandon. And I lost love;

Many times I chose the illusion of victory over the acknowledgment of my weakness. And I lost my truth;

Many times I chose the surface over the depths. And I lost knowledge;

Many times I chose selfishness over generosity. And I lost what I have not given away;

Many times I desperately wanted things which were silly, or vain, or futile, or juvenile, or out of my reach;

The vain things I sought and got only brought me a feeling of ridiculousness;

The out-of-reach things I sought and never got only wasted my time and brought me a feeling of frustration.

... And I learned, and I gained, a lot from each and every loss. From each and every wound. From each and every tear. From each and every fall.

ﻉ

There are still so many things that I would have wished to write about in this book: love, solitude, marriages, divorces, age, relationships, the need for space, the need for intimacy, seizing the moment, testing new things, times of ultimate joy, times of absolute despair ...

Also: the persistent harem syndrome, the virginity myth, the art of multi-tasking, the importance of education, the meaning of a career, the value of financial independence ...

Not to mention: languages, ambitions; me raising my kids, my kids raising me; breaking moulds, transcending formulas ...

But I'm not ready for these topics yet. So they'll have to wait.

I hope you will, too.

In the meantime, here's one last glance at my reality; OUR reality as Arab women: 'Paradoxically, the more the West comes to terms with the gains of modern feminism, and waxes indignant at the "humiliations" to which Arab women are subjected, the less do women in the Arab world itself open their mouths. Today, as the streets of Cairo and Beirut fill once again with women shrouded in black, seeking the respectability of a cloak for their corporeal existence, and fundamentalism wages a triumphant campaign to fix their identity in the mould of religious austerity, many Arab feminists and socialists defend themselves only very timidly against the tide' (Mai Ghoussoub).

The above words have never been more true and accurate.

'Funambulists': no better epithet to describe us Arab women at this time of history. Funambulists hanging in the air, between the sky and the earth, on a cord stretched between misery and deliverance. Moreover, there's no safety net under us.

Yet here I am; here we are: Arab women who 'open their mouths'.

Arab women who 'defend themselves against the tide'.

Arab women who do not put up with things, or spare the others.

Arab women who say NO.

Arab women who, in short, try to cross the abyss.

Will we ever get to the other side, I wonder?

I'll let you know if we do.

I promise.

# To Start Again

*Am I really an 'Arab woman'?*

Dear Westerner,

*And* most importantly: Dear Arab,

Beyond the lure of denial and self-deception, clichés and anti-clichés, the common and the exception, the reality and the mask (and both are fake and deceiving, by the way), now the time has come to ask the following question: is there really such an entity as 'the Arab woman'?

Indeed, whether I like it or not, whether I approve or disapprove of the label, I am a woman, an Arab woman, an Arab woman writer. I symbolise the perfect 'zoo attraction' in the post-9/11 era. But does that have to make me the representative of a 'species'? Believe me when I say I actually barely represent myself.

I am not a fan of sermons. And I most certainly lack the qualifications – and the desire – to lecture others. So please don't perceive my words as a harangue when I say to you: there are so many of us Arab women. Let us not be taken – nor accept to be taken – in handfuls. 'To particularise is the alone distinction of merit' (William Blake). In fact, we've been given nails for a reason: in order to differentiate, to dig deeper, to tear off the generalising, sensationalist skin, and reach for what's beyond the glistening surface ... For 'veils' come in many models and textures: there's the veil of denial; the veil of self-deception; the veil of compromise; the veil of the exotic label; the veil of the biased political message; the veil of the distorted view and extrapolation; the veil of apprehension and fear; the veil of the narrow-minded judgment; and, most dangerously, the veil of the false, media-fabricated symbol ...

Allow me at this point to repeat: not all Arab women lack a backbone. Of that it is proof enough for us, Westerners and Arabs, to read the essays of intellectuals such as May Ziade, Huda Shaarawi, Etel Adnan, Mai Ghoussoub, Fatima Mernissi, Laure Moughaizel and Khalida Said; to discover the novels of writers such as Ahdaf Soueif, Alawiya Sobh, Hoda Barakat, Hanan El Sheikh and Sahar Khalifeh; to see the works of artists such as Zaha Hadid, Mona Hatoum, Helen

Khal and Ghada Amer; to understand the poems of Joyce Mansour, Saniyya Saleh, Nazek Al Mala'ika, Nadia Tueni and Fadwa Touqan; to watch the plays of Jalila Bakkar, Raja' Ben Ammar, Lina Khoury, Darina El Joundi and Nidal Al Ashkar; to enjoy the movies of Jocelyne Saab, Randa Shahhal, Danielle Arbid, Layla Al Marrakshi, and many many others ...

In fact, this testimony is also a modest tribute to all the above-mentioned wonderful writers, thinkers, artists and scholars, and to each and every Arab woman, whether prominent or anonymous, who, despite the numerous challenges, obstacles and threats that face her, still manages to make a difference in life. In hers, thus in ours.

Our misunderstanding, the West's and the East's, is mutual. And I know we Arabs generalise about Westerners even more than they generalise about us (one hideous example is the image of the 'depraved', 'easy', decadent Western woman, which is alas not that uncommon a representation in many Arabs' perceptions). But do we really want to know each other better? Then we need to start believing there is no 'you', and no 'us'. There are no human samples, no stereotypes. Every person and every path in life is unique. Let us seek the nucleus: the whole is comprised in the core. And the core is not static. Its splendour is to be continuously unrecognisable, because continuously in transformation.

ॐ

So do you think you know me by now, having patiently finished this book? Do you think you can corner me in a specific category, having read this testimony?

Think again, because I have drastically changed *while* you were reading.

And so have you.

"Nothing is what it seems," wrote Franz Kafka.

It's about time all of us, Arabs and non-Arabs, East and West, started believing him.

# Post-Partum

## *I Killed Scheherazade*

I've never been a big fan of Scheherazade.

I know that, being an Arab woman and all, I am supposed to be 'in admiration', or at least supportive of her. But I am not.

It might look, at first sight, as if I were jealous of her. Scheherazade this, Scheherazade that: she just pops out of her Pandora's box every time an Arab woman writer is mentioned somewhere in the world. But I am not jealous of her. I can't be. And I'll explain why.

You see, Scheherazade is constantly celebrated in our culture as an educated woman who was resourceful, and imaginative, and intelligent enough to save herself from death by bribing 'the man' with her endless stories. But I've never really liked this 'bribing the man' scheme. For one thing, I believe it sends women the wrong message: 'Persuade men, give them the things that you have and they want, and they'll spare you.' Correct me if I'm wrong, but it seems obvious that this method puts the man in the omnipotent position, and the woman in the compromising, inferior one. It does not teach women resistance and rebellion, as is implied when the character of Scheherazade is discussed and analysed. It rather teaches them concession and nego-tiation over their basic RIGHTS. It persuades them that pleasing the man, whether by a story, or a nice meal, or a pair of silicone tits, or a good fuck, or whatever, is the way to 'make it' in life.

And this is considered inventiveness?

And this is considered resistance?

Call me short-sighted, but I don't think so.

I've never been a big fan of Scheherazade – who, to make matters worse, is nauseatingly cherished by the Oriental-ists – even though I really loved reading and re-reading *The Arabian Nights*. Her character, I am convinced, is a conspiracy against Arab women in particular, and women in general. Obviously, the poor lady did what she had to do. I am not judging her for that. In fact, I might have very well done the same, had I been in her delicate position. I've just had enough of people (especially in the West, but in the

Arab world as well) turning her into a heroin, the symbol of Arab cultural female opposition and struggle against men's injustice, cruelty and discrimination. She's just a sweet gal with a huge imagination and good negotiation skills. Things simply needed to be put into their right perspective.

Thus, I killed her.

≈

I killed Scheherazade. I strangled her with my two bare hands. Someone had to do it, eventually. Counter-analysis and intellectual challenging of her figure were not efficient enough.

And it wasn't that difficult a murder to achieve, to tell you the truth. For instead of trying to fight me back, instead of kicking and scratching and biting, like any reasonably courageous fictional character would have done, that silly woman simply offered to tell me a story in return for sparing her life! Can you believe it? Talk about unavoidable patterns. That, of course, was the fatal blow to her chances. I just couldn't stand it. So I kept on squeezing my hands around her fragile neck until she breathed her last story. Oops, I mean her last breath.

I killed Scheherazade. But I can't take all the credit. Many accomplices have helped me pull off this slaughter along the way; inciters who joined their hands – whether hostile or encouraging – with mine, and that, consequently, I need to gratefully list at this point:

I killed Scheherazade with the hands of all the men who tried, in different ways and under various masks, to slash my throat;

I killed Scheherazade with the hands of all the women who tried, in different ways and under various masks, to make me believe it is OK to have my throat slashed by a man;

I killed Scheherazade with the hands of all the men and women who wanted me to give up a part of myself, in order not to have my throat slashed;

I killed Scheherazade with the hands of every writer forbidden, whether by an outer or an inner censor, to write what he/she felt like writing, and had the right to write;

I killed Scheherazade with the hands of my mother, who did not wish me to have her kind of life, and who made it clear – and possible – right from the start;

I killed Scheherazade with the hands of my father, who, from being afraid for me, became proud of me, although the road in between was a very hard one;

I killed Scheherazade with the hands of the different religious representatives and leaders, who made me realise the gap between authenticity and blind adherence to anything;

I killed Scheherazade with the hands of the numerous stiff conservatives I met in my life, who made me discover the difference between everlasting human ethics and futile values;

I killed Scheherazade with the hands of the Calvin Klein models, the James Bond girls, and every woman who is treated like a delicious piece of meat in magazines, movies, on TV screens and in real life;

I killed Scheherazade with the hands of every teenager who starves herself to death because she was brainwashed to believe men will like her better this way;

I killed Scheherazade with the hands of every man who was laughed at by his Neanderthal macho friends because he treats women decently;

I killed Scheherazade with the hands of the doctor who slapped me when I came out of my mother's womb, and each person who slapped me – or tried to – after that;

I killed Scheherazade with the hands of my maths teacher in fourth grade, who wanted to convince me that boys were good with numbers, and girls with cooking;

I killed Scheherazade with the hands of every Barbie doll polluting the mind of every little girl in every city around the world;

I killed Scheherazade with the hands of every scream I did not dare to scream, and every NO I did not dare – yet – to say;

I killed Scheherazade with the hands of every friend who betrayed me, and every friend I betrayed;

I killed Scheherazade with the hands of every victory I witnessed, and every defeat I survived;

I killed Scheherazade with the hands of every person I have been, every person I am now, and every person I will be;

And, last but not least, I killed Scheherazade with the hands of Lilith: my seed, my root, my earth and my truth.

Yes, I killed Scheherazade. I killed her in me. And I am quite determined to kill everything and everyone that even remotely looks or behaves like her in my unconscious, imagination and mind. So her sisters, daughters, grand-daughters and all her descendants had better close down the concessions' business, or stay away, far away from me.

For there's an angry Arab woman out there. She's got her own 'not-intended-for-negotiation' stories, her own 'not-granted-by-anybody' freedom and life,
   *and* the perfect murder weapon.

And there's no stopping her now.

# The Poet's Chapter

*Attempt at an Autobiography*

## GEOLOGY OF THE I

A poem is a naked person
*Bob Dylan*

I am the sixth day of December of the year 1970;
I am the hour just after noon.
I am my mother's screams giving birth to me
and her screams giving birth to her.
Her womb releasing me to emerge from myself,
her sweat achieving my potentiality.
I am the doctor's slap which revived me.
(Each subsequent slap trying to revive me quite destroyed
     me.)
I am the eyes of the family upon me,
the gazes of father, grandfather, of aunts.

I am all their possible scenarios;

I am the curtains drawn, the curtains behind the curtains
   and the walls behind those,

and I am she who has no name, no hand, for what comes
   behind.

I am the expectations of me, the aborted dreams,

the voids suspended as amulets around my neck.

I am the tight red coat I cried whenever I wore,

and every constriction which still makes me cry.

I am the brown-haired doll with plastic eyes;

I am that discarded doll I refused to rock,

cast aside, still oozing blood from the base of the head,

(Two drops on ordinary days and three on days off and
   holidays).

I am the sad hole in my teacher's socks.

It still stares at me like the reproach of Abel in my soul,

staring to tell me of her poverty and my impotence,

the exhaustion of my patience and the terror of her
   despair.

I am the times table I haven't mastered to this day;

I am the two that adds up to one, always one.

I am the theory of curved lines, never joined up,

and I am their applications.

I am my hatred of history, of algebra and of physics.

I am my faith, as a child, that the earth revolved around
   my heart

and my heart around the moon.

I am the lie of Santa Claus,

which I believe to this day.

I am the astronaut I used to dream I would become.

I am the wrinkles of my grandmother who committed
    suicide;

I am my forehead leaning on her absent lap.

I am the boy (was he called Jack?) who pulled my hair and
    ran off.

I am he who made me cry, which made me love him even
    more.

I

am my little kitten;

and the neighbours' son's bicycle which ran me over and I
    did not protest.

(I sold the souls of my cat for a single glance from that
    handsome boy.)

I am blackmail, my inaugural vice.

I am war

and the corpse of the man the combatants dragged around
    in front of me,

and his torn up leg trying to catch up with him.

I

am the books which I read as a child which were unsuitable
    for me,

(Which I now write and which are still unsuitable for
    me).
I am the adolescence of my right breast,
and I am the wisdom of the left.
The power of both under a tight shirt
and then my awareness of their power: the beginning of
    the descent.
I am my rapid boredom, my first cigarette, my late
    obstinacy,
and the seasons past.
I am the granddaughter of the child I was;
her lack of my anger,
my disappointments and my triumphs,
my labyrinths and my lusts,
my lies, my wars,
my scars and my wrong turns.
I am the tenderness I bear despite myself;
I am my god and my greed;
my absences filled with my dead;
and I am my dead who never sleep,
my slain who never sleep;
I am their last sighs on the pillow each dawn.
And I
am my resentment, my contagion,
my danger,
and my flight from cowardice to worse.

I am my waiting around not knowing the time
and my not understanding space.
I am the silence which I have learned
and the silence which I haven't mastered yet.
The solitude which steps on my soul like an insect.
I am the granddaughter of the child I was:
My lack of her innate carelessness,
of her selfless perfection.
I am love's disaster
and happening.
I am the wolf of poetry coursing through my blood
and me running barefoot with it;
I am she who is in search of her hunter
not finding her hunter.
I am the frothing waters of my lust as it gestures onto
     lust;
I am the succession of tongues which irrigate its froth,
and my lipstick anticipating their thirst.
I am my fingernails too: what lies beneath them and what
     they sink into.
I am the memory of their wounds,
the memory of their anger,
the memory of their weakness,
the memory of their strength, beyond proof,
and I am the little pieces of flesh torn from men's backs
in each ecstatic moment.

I am my teeth

and my delicate thighs

and my bawdy desires.

I am my sins and oh how I love them;

I am my sins and the way they mirror me.

And I am my girlfriend who betrayed me –

And I thank her for that.

I am my spinal cord howling in the face of the traitors.

I am my eyes looking into a darkness which is mine.

I am my pain,

yes, my pain.

I am my scream in the middle of the night

(suppressed at the appropriate time).

I am what they tell me not to say

not to dream

not to think

not to dare

not to take.

I am what they tell me not to be.

I am what I hide,

what I don't want to hide but do

and what I do want to hide and don't.

I am 'tell me how much you love me'

and 'I don't believe you.'

I am the head connected to the body, disconnected from
     the body.

I am my early death – I say that without drama –
and whatever devastation will be left behind me.
I am the madness and the absence which are before me
And the petty, little, revealing things:
The postage stamps, the clippings from letters,
the notes under the glass of the table, my smiles in old
  photos.
I am the composite of men who loved me and whom I
  didn't love.
I am those I loved who didn't love me,
those I didn't love and who didn't love me,
and those who imagined I loved them
and imagined that they didn't love me.
I am the composite of the one man whom I love.
I am the bride whose image cried in the photo of her first
  wedding (but only the image).
I am my refractions, my defeats, my vain victories.
I am my salvation from drowning once (if it really was
  salvation).
I am the staleness of a breadcrumb on my table.
I am the seven days and the centuries which it took me to
  create myself.
I am the fish and the birds and the trees
and the smoke of the factories,
and the asphalt of the road and the whistling of the
  bombs,

and I am the wind and the spiders and the flesh of fruit.
I am every volcano on top of every mountain in every
    country on every continent on every planet.
I am each hole dug in the earth of each country on each
    continent on each planet.
I am the second which it took me to destroy myself
and all my bodies
and the humid streets of my city
and I am who I was and I am who I could have been.

I am the blue dress that my mother refused to buy for herself
    so as to pay my school fees.
I am my father's library, his eyes and his petulant heart.
I am the glances I did not allow myself, the words I did not
    say and the lips I did not kiss
and the trails I will not leave behind me:
All the stupid things I did not do
all the great things I haven't done yet
all the departures I did not return from.
I
am my daughter whom I did not give birth to
whom I might
and
the woman I will be.
I am almost that woman
and I am almost the man

that I did not become completely
that I don't want to become
and who saves me from myself every day.
I am the woman that I am not right now,
all the things and the people who I was yesterday,
who I will be tomorrow,
and who create
uncreate
recreate me.

# Acknowledgments

I firstly thank all the wonderful friends who took the time to read my modest text, and gave me insightful remarks and useful comments to improve it. These are (in alphabetical order): Akl Awit, Etel Adnan, Luca Bonaccorsi, Oriana Capezio, Peter Carlsson, Hala Habib, Marilyn Hacker, Renée Hayek, Schona Jolly, Stephen McCormick and Jan Henrik Swahn.

I also thank the great inspiring women (*and* men) in my culture, as well as the great inspiring women (*and* men) in the whole world. Those I quoted, and those whose unquoted, yet very much present, words motivate me every step of the way; those who came and went away, those who are still here, and those who are yet to come. I owe to all of them who I am, and mostly, what I am still to become.

Last but not least, I thank my parents for their qualities and their flaws, for their moments of doubt and faith in me, for the achievements and mistakes they made, for the right and wrong words they said, for what they took and what they gave, for messing me up and for helping me out, often simultaneously. And I thank my two sons, Mounir and Ounsi, for teaching me every day how to deserve them more, as a mother, as a woman and as a human being.

J.H.